CHOOSE to be
FIERCELY JOYFUL !!

Tasha
Drutkins

FIERCELY JOYFUL

11 KEYS TO LIVING AUTHENTICALLY & CREATING A LIFE YOU LOVE

NATASHA CRAIG DURKINS

MANUSCRIPTS
PRESS

FIERCELY JOYFUL
11 Keys to Living Authentically & Creating a Life You Love

ISBN   979-8-88926-766-9   *Paperback*
           979-8-88926-525-2   *Hardcover*
           979-8-88926-767-6   *Ebook*

To Edwaun, Chicago's finest and my biggest champion, you support every dream I have. Life with you is beautiful.

To my family, thank you for supporting me always.

To Mom and Dad, I miss you, thank you for being amazing, and I hope you're proud.

To everyone who wants to be more of themselves and seeks greater fulfillment in life, I wrote this for you.

CONTENTS

INTRODUCTION

"The place in which I'll fit will not exist until I make it."

—JAMES BALDWIN

You may believe conformity is a must to have a place in this world. We often see fitting in as the best road to success and happiness. Gotta play the game to win the game, right? I'm here to tell you there's a new way to play, and it's not about fitting into a box someone else created for you. Yes, we can appreciate having some structure to start with. And sure, we can design the inside of the box. But y'all, it's *still a damn box*. I don't wanna be in one. I am not playing small for anydamnbody. I was created to be uniquely me, and you were created to be uniquely you. What's the purpose of being unique if no one gets to experience it?

Because I lost Mom and Dad when I was young (twenty when mom died and twenty-nine when Dad died), I've spent years reflecting on what they gave me—intangible gifts that helped me become the woman I am today. I'm not perfect. I'm proud—of who I am and the work I continue to do to be the best version of me. I'm full of joy and fulfilled, which is better than perfect any day.

I'm grateful for the exposure I had outside of my own world: volunteering, Broadway plays (ever stand in line early in the morning in NYC for same-day tickets? Best memories ever!), dive/hole-in-the-wall dining, museums, swimming, politics, art, activism, being in community with others, and so much more. I learned how much opportunity the world offers, which inspired and motivated me to achieve goals seemingly beyond my grasp. I learned, too, it's not all about me. Pretty important lesson. Now, don't get it twisted. What I want and need matters—it's just not the *only* thing that matters. We have a responsibility to our fellow citizens of the world.

I recognize the gifts Mom and Dad gave me aren't just mine. I want and feel a responsibility to pay it forward. Many people lose their parents too soon. I'm one of millions. But the years I had were wonderful and foundational. From my parents, I learned *how to be*. Coincidentally, this is the name of an etiquette book I love because I admire the person Harriette Cole describes in *How to Be: A Guide for Contemporary Living for African Americans* (2000).

The excitement I feel when I remember the amazing experiences I've had makes me smile from the inside out. When I share my stories, it helps people look at life through a different lens, leading to finding happiness and joy by design. I help people recognize what they see as impossible, isn't.

Everyone deserves a life they love. The major obstacle to getting there is the person staring back at us in the mirror. Chiefly, it's the stories we tell ourselves and those we adopt from someone else's judgment, often holding us back from pushing past discomfort or fear. There is much more within our own control than we tend to acknowledge. It's the ability to *choose* that empowers us to create a life we love. It's there by default. Our role is to summon the courage to use our power of choice. Allow me to repeat: *you choose*. Not Mom or Dad, not your partner, not your BFF, not your mentor, not your sibling, not society. *You.*

It took me so many years to get here. Now, don't be mistaken: "here" isn't a place of perfection. I have bad days like everyone else. Some things in my life are not quite what I want them to be (to name one, the need to wear Spanx with formfitting dresses, but I digress). Still, I'm filled with joy and gratitude for the life I designed without intention for many years, and now with. I only wish I had the knowledge, understanding, lessons learned, and courage to get "here" much sooner. I've written this book to share how good *being you* can feel and how it helps make your life one you love.

This book is for you. Yes, *you*. The one who bites her tongue. The one who tries so hard to please everyone *except* himself. The one who shows up for everyone *except* herself. The one who pretends to be happy when sad. The one who says yes when his inner voice is shouting no. The one who never accepts help when it's offered but bends over backward helping others. The one who puts her needs after everyone else's. The one who tries to be what their parents want rather than what they yearn to be. The one who puts dreams on hold. The one who self-eliminates. The one who cries alone. The one surrounded by family and friends yet feels an overwhelming sense of loneliness. The one who pretends to like things they don't. The one who's afraid to be vulnerable. The one who dismisses how their uniqueness makes them absolutely amazing.

In this book, I'll share with you the keys enabling me to live a life rooted in who I truly am. *Fiercely Joyful* will help you understand what living authentically means, why it's important, and how to do it. I will share stories and tools to help you show up as who you truly are so you can create a life you absolutely love.

Too many of us find ourselves in the space of settling for our life instead of creating the one we want. Many people say they're living authentically. Are you when being authentic only serves others, not yourself? I will help you achieve *true* and *complete* authenticity that gets you much closer to self-actualization.

I've gained a sense of joy and fulfillment that comes from being authentic and giving myself some grace and compassion. I created a life I love in which I'm willing to take risks, try new things, fail, learn, grow, and embrace what life has to offer. This work isn't only about the destination. So, c'mon and take the journey with me. We're going to enjoy it together on your way to becoming *Fiercely Joyful*.

1

BECOMING ME

My childhood is amazing in so many ways. My friends and the community love my parents. They have huge hearts and deep beliefs in social responsibility. Both Mom and Dad have big personalities, though they present quite differently. People are in awe of Mom's kindness, thoughtfulness, and compassion. She remembers birthdays, shows up for important events (gifts in hand), and feeds more friends in our home than all the restaurants in Scranton, Pennsylvania, can hold. Dad's gregariousness, sense of humor, and positivity attracts the world to him. Hanging out with Dad is always memorable, whether at a hole-in-the-wall café along the highway or watching *Dreamgirls* on Broadway in New York City. You'll end the day knowing you'll never forget it.

It's not only who they are shaping me and my brother Ellis, but also what they do. Mom and Dad expose us to the world beyond our own. They want us to see and experience it for ourselves—the good and the bad. Understanding what's out there gives us perspective and prepares us for life's challenges. We often volunteer, supporting those less fortunate. We take trips on Amtrak to Washington,

DC, visiting museums and monuments. We visit our local zoo and gain an appreciation for animals and go to Dad's favorite used bookstore for our nonacademic books.

We participate in protests and marches in support of equal rights. We shop at both the Goodwill and the Globe, our upscale neighborhood department store. We go to lectures at the University of Scranton. We spend time on farms (I try opting out to no avail), on the West Coast, and in the South. And we work a steady job from the age of thirteen. Allowance from chores around the house is eliminated as soon as we're hired, so we get a better idea of what it takes to earn money. Over my teenage years, I worked at Dad's warehouse cleaning used kitchen equipment (yuck), serving scoops in the ice cream parlor he opens, bus tables in the restaurant he owns, and being a parking attendant for a lot he leased (so boring yet it's easy money!).

The sturdy foundation upon which I'm built as a human being matters most in who I've become. Let's take a walk down memory lane so I can share experiences along my journey to a fiercely joyful life.

THEY PAVE THE WAY

Some of the happiest times of my childhood are spent with the women in my family. They are phenomenal. Aunt Dorothy is a pioneer and teaches me how to be determined and brave. Aunt Charlotte cherishes laughter and shows me how to be compassionate and thoughtful to my loved ones. Aunt Liz reminds me not to take life too seriously and to look for silver linings. Aunt Claudia transforms my hair into a work of art while making sure I understand beauty comes from the inside out. Aunt Teddy calls me Miss America and introduces me to building community by opening up her home. How fortunate I am to have role models in my family demonstrating the power of *us*.

My family calls me an old soul. I much prefer spending time with my mom and her girlfriends than with friends my age. I'm all up in their conversations. I love listening to and learning from Mom and Nana (my maternal grandmother), especially during our Saturday shopping outings. We're just running errands and grabbing a bite to eat along the way, though I experience it as so much more.

We always make three stops: McCrory's, Woolworths, and Kmart. Sometimes, we go to a dollar store and the Goodwill, too, which is Nana's favorite. My job is to push the cart while Mom and Nana fill it. Checking out clothing is a must at every store. I love when Mom asks my opinion about things she likes, though it's rare she buys something for herself. She's more interested in things my brother Ellis and I need.

Throughout the day, my ears stay tuned in. I don't want to miss a thing from Mom and Nana's conversations. I learn what they believe about life and *why*. Hearing those conversations helped me learn *how to be*. What sticks with me still:

- Our words matter
- We must own our mistakes
- We teach people how to treat us
- We must keep our word
- Kindness isn't optional
- Give loved ones flowers while they're here to receive them

These courageous, remarkable women give me a sense of my own value and what I must do to maintain it. What I learn and how it influences the trajectory of my authentic life is priceless.

ON BEING FIERCELY JOYFUL

"The beautiful thing about learning is nobody can take it away from you."

—B.B. KING

What I learn from the matriarchs of my family is timeless wisdom I treasure. I hold it close and remember it. Something else the family collective teaches me is to extend my hand, lifting others up as I climb. Not only should I cherish and use my learning, I should share it. It'll always be there for me, *and* it can be there for you too. Thus, I present to you, *Fiercely Joyful.*

BREAKING HEARTS

About the time I entered my teens, my parents' marriage became rocky. I cringe when I hear the yelling. Sometimes I whip my head so sharply when one of them utters nasty and disrespectful words, it catches their attention. They exchange glances, lower their eyes, and abruptly stop.

Dad is a workaholic, and he doesn't spend much time with us and Mom. He shows up for some of my brother Ellis's football games. When I look out into the audience with hope after my dance recitals and school debates, my shoulders drop seeing Mom next to an empty seat. The evening a kid rings our doorbell in the middle of dinner is when I learn we have a half brother who's close to my age. Shock and disbelief draw silent tears when he says, "Hi, I'm your brother Isaac." Mom's head moves left to right, her breath quickens, and she's shaking. She doesn't look surprised though, and over the years we gain more half brothers and sisters.

One day, I notice my parents' closet is half empty, signaling the beginning of their years-long separation. Dad's behavior breaks Mom's heart and mine. I'm angry at Dad and sad for Mom when the divorce finally comes. She trembles in my arms with puffy eyes, mourning the end of the life she's known for nearly two decades.

Dad leaves Scranton, Pennsylvania, where we lived, and moves to Montego Bay, Jamaica. There, he starts a new business and a new family. Our relationship becomes strained. I'm hurt not only by his infidelity but how he left Mom to fend for herself, not even paying enough child support to cover the bills. We go from school field trips, Broadway shows, and dance classes to Mom struggling to pay utilities and buy groceries with the money she earns in a week. Though I tell Dad we need help, he insists, "Trust me, I'm sending your mom plenty of money." Eventually, I give up and stop talking to him about it. Mom, Ellis, and I work together as a team to find our way. It requires sacrifice—no more dance classes, no more class trips. Somehow, Mom makes sure we have what we *need*.

My relationship with Dad is estranged for a time after the divorce when he is mostly absent from our lives. He flies in from Jamaica and asks me to join him for a quick road trip to New Jersey. On the drive back to DC, I can't stop thinking about how he betrayed Mom. I want to know Dad regrets the choices he made which tore our family apart. I take a deep breath, push past the pit in my stomach, and ask, "Dad, are you sorry for being unfaithful to Mom?" As his immediate tirade ensues, my entire body starts shaking. His fiery words leave spit on the windshield. My heartbeat hits its max when the car swerves from him pounding on the steering wheel. *Oh my God, I have never seen Dad so angry.* I can't muster a single word in response as I wipe my wet cheeks. Unable to look at him, I turn my head toward the window until the agonizing ride is over.

Dad isn't going to own his mistakes. I have to choose whether I can get over it. I'm proud of myself for saying something rather than seething quietly about it. If I hadn't already lost Mom, I don't know whether my decision would have been the same. But the fact is, I only have one parent left. I know in my soul it's more important for me to have Dad in my life than for me to convince him to own his shit. I move on again, but this time it's my intentional choice to do so.

ON BEING FIERCELY JOYFUL

"Forgiveness isn't approving what happened. It's choosing to rise above it."

—ROBIN SHARMA

With 100 percent certainty, I can tell you today I made the right decision. Continuing to have Dad in my life, focusing on the greatest parts of the man he was, enriched me beyond measure. I can't imagine my life without the happier experiences we had together after the blowup. We all have a loved one who has behaved in a way we believe is unforgivable. You have to decide for yourself whether it ends there, or you surrender and forgive.

I'm not a grudge holder. It doesn't serve me well because I gain nothing from it, and I don't want to surrender the amount of energy it requires to carry a grudge. I'd rather surrender the negativity, which is why I choose to forgive. Before I learned forgiving others shows compassion for myself, I'd carry the anger around like a weighty backpack. I dragged it around because I thought it was hitting back at the offender. You know—an *I'll show them* type of thing. Meanwhile, the offending person is living life and not thinking 'bout me and my anger even a tiny bit. Y'all know it's true! Consider lightening your load, breathing in some peace, and breathing out negative feelings.

***

FIGURING THINGS OUT

It's the early 1990s, and I'm in my second semester at Howard University when Mom notices a lump on her lower back. She visits her doctor, who tells her it's a benign cyst, and he schedules a procedure to remove it. When Mom's doctor begins the procedure and sees the tissue, he immediately realizes it's not a benign mass after all. Tests later reveal it's lymphoma. I'm upset the doctor didn't do a biopsy before the procedure. Did he make things worse? I don't know for sure, but the unsettling feeling in my spirit doesn't go away.

I leave school and go home to care for Mom. She undergoes chemotherapy, then radiation, and has surgery aimed at removing the cancer. Being an eighteen-year-old caregiver is so hard, but I do my best. I'm home for about nine months until Mom gets better. Her hair starts growing back, she's energetic again, and even enrolls in college to pursue her bachelor's degree. I'm so proud of her! I'm also excited to go back to DC with my friends and get back into school.

Mom continues to do well for several months, and we expect good news from her next checkup. Instead, we learn Mom's body is again under attack. The lymphoma is not only back, it's spreading aggressively. Mom has two more surgeries and more chemo, but the cancer moves to her organs. There's nothing more they can do. I receive a call one evening after class from my mom's brother telling me I should consider coming home because Mom isn't improving. I hang up the phone, sink to the floor, and bury my head in my hands as I pray for a different outcome.

A couple of weeks after I'm back home, Mom calls a family meeting. Dad flies in from Jamaica. Despite our awkward silence and lowered heads, with a sense of calm easing us all, she shares her wishes and tells Dad she needs him to be there for us after she's gone. He commits to it. After the meeting is over, Mom hands me her bible. "Look at the inside of the back cover." I find a list of what she wants for her funeral. My throat aches, and my body tenses as I read it and wonder why this is happening to us. I'm so grateful for it six weeks later when Mom takes her last breath. I don't have to spend a moment thinking about what songs should be sung, what scriptures should be read, or even how to dress Mom in her casket. She blessed me with all the answers before I even knew what the questions would be.

I dismiss my family's advice a couple of days before the funeral and cut my shoulder-length hair into a very short and tapered style. The morning of Mom's homegoing, I step into the black pinstripe skirt suit I bought and imagine it's my protective armor. With my eyes closed, I straighten my back and lift my chin as the procession begins. Teardrops full of anguish disappear into my new suit with each step I take.

After nearly two years of being my mom's caregiver, I learn I have to count on *me* to get things done. My family expects me to be strong, to know what needs to be done, and to make it happen. I did and started figuring things out on my own.

ON BEING FIERCELY JOYFUL

"She needed a hero, so that's what she became."

—ANONYMOUS

Sometimes in life, we are the only ones we can rely on. It's not ideal but may be unavoidable. Mom reminded me of this after she and Dad divorced. She relied so heavily on him, she felt helpless when he left. She didn't know how to manage money, didn't have a career outside of the family business (which she didn't want to reference), and she had no income or savings other than what Dad gave her. I took her advice to heart, and over time found a way to balance my individual ability to thrive with sharing a life with my husband Edwaun in which we rely on one another. Find what works for you, and be prepared to be your own hero when life demands it.

THE PAST RETURNS

There's a lot of my childhood I don't recall. For a long time, I chalk it up to having a poor memory. I later learn it's the result of repressing experiences I want to forget. About two years after Mom dies, horrific memories return to the surface.

I wake up startled, shaking, and nauseous. So much I'd buried so deeply within me is flooding to the surface in what feels like a single moment. I'm watching my mind's movie reel. Each scene is painful. I can see the past clearly, as if it all just happened. My body shakes with panic, anger, and sadness while I cry uncontrollably off and on for hours. I now have to reckon with my truth.

Grandad molests me from about age nine to fourteen. Not sure where the courage comes from, but one day, I decide it has to stop. I avoid at all costs going alone to my grandparents' home. Grandad seems unafraid of being caught since he even molests me when Nana is home. They sleep in separate bedrooms, which makes it easier for him to get to me. Still, I'm certain he won't be able to ever touch me again if I never go into his room alone. When he calls me to come into his room, knots form in my stomach. I tell myself, *I can do this... I can do this.* I walk toward his room and plant my feet firmly outside his door with my head held high. Without saying a word, I tell him it's over, and I never pass the threshold to his room again. You see, Grandad is in a wheelchair. He cannot walk. Because it's a manual wheelchair, his hands and arms are incredibly strong. Whenever he grabbed me, I was never able to peel his fingers away. I withdraw from Grandad both physically and emotionally. Our relationship is reduced to hellos and goodbyes, and I'm so grateful he won't hurt me again.

Grandad always said it was my fault because I gave him indications I "wanted it." I believe him. I'm searching my mind relentlessly trying to remember what I did so I can make sure I never do it again. I don't say out loud what he's done. I'm scared because I worry Grandad is right when he says I'll get in trouble if anyone finds out what I did.

I know my mom would believe me. There are so many times I almost tell her, but my tongue stiffens, and my lips refuse to open. I believe Grandad molested Mom, too, because she asks me now and then after I get back from my grandparents' apartment whether anything unusual happened. I lie and say no. I don't want to upset my mom. It will break her heart, so it's best to keep it a secret and focus on staying away from him.

After I stop my grandfather from molesting me, I don't expect it to happen to me ever again because I know what to do now. Unfortunately, I learn soon I'm still vulnerable. I had the same babysitter for as long as I can remember. Our two families are very close, and she lives steps away from us. When I'm old enough to not need a babysitter anymore, we become more like friends, and I love hanging out with her at her house after school. One day, she forces me to perform sexual acts on her. I run home as soon as it's over. I shower, scrubbing my skin until it's red, and then cry myself to sleep. In the morning, I can't look at myself in the mirror. I think about how Grandad said I sent him signals and worry I'm doing it again with her. Accepting fault for what happened, I'm sure it's only a onetime thing. *She won't do it again because after it was over, she can tell I didn't want it, right?* Wrong. It happens several more times until I sever the friendship. She realizes I'm angry and convinces me no one will believe me if I tell. Once again, I keep the secret.

I can't believe, yet again, a person I love and treated like family became someone I hate with every part of my being. I stop going to her house and cut her off completely. From time to time, Mom asks what happened. I tell her we grew apart. Years later, my former babysitter marries and has a child. I want to run to the police station and ask them to watch her to make sure she doesn't do to her child what she did to me. My gut tells me she is sick enough to do it. I'm angry at myself for not telling on her, always worrying about her son and praying I am wrong.

When I'm seventeen, about a year after Nana dies, Grandad is hospitalized. I'm a two-hour drive away from home on a college tour when Mom calls to say he won't survive much longer. She lets me decide whether to come home to see him. I ask her to come get me so I can say goodbye. By the time I get to the hospital, Grandad isn't talking anymore, but I sense his mind is still with us.

He extends his hand toward mine. I pause. *I promised myself I would never let him touch me again.* My face turns flush as my spirit tells me it's time to forgive him. The devil on my shoulder isn't having it, shouting in my head, "He doesn't deserve it!" The angel on my other shoulder tells me this is important not for him, but *for me.* Suddenly, calmness envelopes me. It's time to surrender my anger, and I get to do it on my terms. I step back so he can't reach my hand. Then, I look directly into his eyes and whisper, "I forgive you." Grandad dies in the middle of the night. I'm not sad to see him go. I feel relief. The anger has been such a burden not worth carrying.

ON BEING FIERCELY JOYFUL

"By far the strongest poison to the human spirit is the inability to forgive oneself or another person. Forgiveness is no longer an option but a necessity for healing."

—CAROLINE MYSS

If you don't take the time to acknowledge and heal from your past, you'll struggle to live fully in the present. What I need you to take away from this is the trauma you experience in life *does not* define you. It *grows you*. And your healing helps you help others.

THE JOURNEY TO AUTHENTICITY BEGINS

In the days after I wake up remembering the past, I'm angry about the burden I've been carrying subconsciously for so long. I'm angry at myself for listening when people told me to push past my hurt, to move on. We *have to* experience the hurt, pain, struggles—the hard things—so we can heal and then recognize and enjoy the wonderful things. I resent my family expected me to keep a brave face after Mom died. No one encouraged me to allow myself to grieve. Holding it all in is unhealthy.

With this revelation, I decide I'm not going to hide my hurt anymore. It is much more important for me to work through pain or trauma than to make others feel comfortable. No more suffering in silence. This is one of my first big forays into living authentically. I acknowledge my loved ones didn't intend to make me suffer in silence. To some extent, we grew up being taught to shrug things off and keep going. They love me and give me the best counsel they can.

It's spring of 1997 when I call my dad and my brothers and tell them I want to have a conference call. I tell them about Grandad, my babysitter, and being raped by my first boyfriend. They're devastated and angry with the perpetrators. Some of the weight eases from my shoulders after I tell my family what happened to me. I'm learning the importance of being honest with my loved ones about my emotions and my mental state. I will not keep painful secrets.

You know how people walk by on the street and say, "How are you?" and we often automatically respond with, "Fine, thanks." It's okay to do with strangers if you want. It's not okay to do with your loved ones. And, if you're super transparent like me, you might not do it with your colleagues. I'm fortunate to work with colleagues who care about me. When my face or mood isn't quite right, they check on me.

I believe if I don't answer truthfully, I might miss out on a blessing for me or someone else. No sir, not doing that! I'll accept any blessing meant to come my way, thank you kindly. Now calm down, answering truthfully doesn't mean you have to do tell-all sessions (unless you wanna, and if you do, more power to ya!). But, it's totally okay to go from "Fine, thanks" to "You know, I'm a little overwhelmed right now while we're planning for my daughter to go to college next year. There's so much to do and a ton of decisions to make." See? Not bad, right? Chances are others will be able to empathize. Or if you want to be honest but less specific, you might say, "I've had better days." People will know you've got some things going on—whether personally or professionally—and they can be sensitive to it. Wouldn't it be great to know it's a bad day for your employee before you tell them they're not meeting your expectations? You might opt to give him some grace and hold the conversation for another day.

ON BEING FIERCELY JOYFUL

"Authenticity means erasing the gap between what you firmly believe and what you reveal to the outside world."

—ADAM GRANT

You lose some of you when you're not authentic. Changing you to make others happy, to fit in, or whatever the rationale, chips away at your soul. Plus, pretending to be someone you aren't is *unbelievably exhausting*. It drains you. Your energy is put to better use spending time with loved ones, making important decisions at work, exercising, or anything else important to you. Pretending for others can lead to pretending for yourself too. Eventually, you can lose sight of what's really happening on the inside. Please y'all, don't do that to you. *You deserve better.*

FROM GRIEF TO GROWTH TO GOWN

After Mom's affairs are settled, I head back to Washington, DC, because Scranton doesn't feel like home without Mom. In the days and months after she passes away, I'm overcome with emotions. Fear, anxiety, and sadness envelope me from head to toe. I'm weighed down. How will I make it through life without her? There's so much I don't know about this world, about myself... about *how to be.* I know my mom, my best friend in the entire world, would expect me to find my way, but I have no clue how. I drop out of college and, for nearly a year, sleep all day long and stay up all night watching the TV shopping networks, ordering things I don't need. When the phone rings, I don't answer because I prefer isolation to socializing. I'm paying my bills with my portion of the insurance money mom left for us.

With the money dwindling and nothing to show for what I've spent, I have to pull myself together and get a job so I can continue to make ends meet. I work a few retail positions and then land a position as a customer service professional for *USA Today*. It's the first time I have a nine-to-five job—no more shift work means I can go back to school.

About five years after Mom's death, I enroll in a two-year degree program at Northern Virginia Community College and then transfer to George Mason University to complete my coursework toward earning my Bachelor of Science in Marketing. As I near the end of my final semester in late 2004, I'm sad Mom isn't alive to see this day. Graduation day isn't until next May, but I'm done with my classes in December. So excited Dad will see me in my cap and gown.

I'm driving home from work when my oldest brother, Gino, calls. On October 12, 2004, nine years after Mom's death, Gino tells me Dad's heart stopped pumping in the middle of a parking lot and he died instantly. My body numbs like I'm frozen in time. Not remembering the rest of the drive, I'm not sure how I made it back to my apartment.

At home, tears flow uncontrollably. I think to myself, *Both of my parents gone?* I'm grateful for my circle of close friends coming over to offer support and comfort. I wake up puffy-eyed the next day realizing I cried myself to sleep. Sitting on my bed, I'm wondering again, *What am I supposed to do with my life? I'm alone with no one to guide me and no parent to care for me.*

Unlike Mom, Dad doesn't have life insurance or any savings, which leaves me and my brother Ellis scrounging up money to pay for Dad's funeral and burial. There is hurtful family drama from those who remember the days when

Dad picked up the tab for dinners, shows, and vacations, put a wad of cash into someone's hand, and lived in a beautiful home in Jamaica with a full-time housekeeper who cooked, cleaned, and helped with the kids from Dad's new family. High streams of income are a thing of the past for Dad. The idea he has plenty of money when he dies is so far from the truth.

Dad has many ebbs and flows in business over the years. His high point is when he signs a contract with UPS. They buy out his Mail Boxes Etc. franchises across the island, and he enters into an agreement to oversee UPS's new Caribbean Division. Dad's company earns seven figures, but a couple of years into the agreement, he believes his share of the profits isn't on par with his contributions. He takes UPS to court to increase his earnings. Dad loses the case and UPS severs the agreement. Between the loss and the hefty legal fees he now has to pay, Dad loses his businesses and his home. He leaves Jamaica for good with no assets and heads to Florida, hoping to get back on his feet.

I ask Dad for his new address. "I'll get it to you." When I can't get a straight answer from Dad about where he's living, it finally hits me. *Oh my God. He doesn't have a place to live?* I keep pressing him in our conversations until he jokes about a car being a much more comfortable place to sleep than one would think.

My mind rewinds and replays the conversations over and over. *Did Dad go from being a millionaire to being homeless?* Living check to check myself limits my ability to help, but I have sixty dollars to spare. "Dad, where can I send you a card?" I mail it to a post office box with a sixty-dollar check enclosed. My father, who has *never* accepted money from me before, cashes the check. My heart sinks, and I know with certainty he is struggling. Fortunately, nothing ever keeps him down for long. His entrepreneurial spirit kicks in, and he starts a used equipment sales business once again. He's able to rent a condo from a longtime friend and is sustaining.

As we prepare for Dad's funeral, family members call asking about his belongings. My temperature is boiling—*are they seriously looking for money and things to be given to them rather than recognizing the difficulty we feel reconciling with Dad's death?* There isn't any money to pay for Dad's casket, let alone cash to divvy out.

Without a will, we can't do anything with the massive amounts of used equipment inventory Dad has in a few warehouses in the Fort Lauderdale area unless we hire an attorney to help get us appointed as Dad's estate executors. Another expense we can't afford; the equipment sits untouched until the state claims it. After having a stroke the year before, Dad warned me our family members would behave this way when he died. I didn't believe it, so I'm not prepared when it happens. I walk away from those who accuse Ellis and me of taking Dad's nonexistent assets and keeping them for ourselves. I've since forgiven but won't forget.

Back home after the funeral, I have final exams to prepare for, yet the only thing I do is sit on the couch watching TV and feeling sorry for myself. A little voice in my head says, *Have you forgotten how hard you worked and sacrificed to earn your degree?* Mom and Dad would be disappointed if I let it slip through my fingers. One day at a time, I press forward, telling myself I only need to worry about "showing up" today because I don't have enough in me to worry about tomorrow. Weeks later, I submit my final paper and complete my capstone project. Degree earned.

ON BEING FIERCELY JOYFUL

I still don't know how I'm going to get through this life on my own and finally realize that's okay. Who has all the answers anyway? What I do know is I have a foundation as solid as the rock of Gibraltar. The foundation gives me the tools I need to not just survive but to eventually thrive. As Dr. Maya Angelou said, "My mission in life is not merely to survive, but to thrive; and to do so with some passion, some compassion, some humor, and some style" (Angelou 2011). She also said, "Surviving is important. Thriving is elegant" (Douglas 2016, 40). Being fiercely joyful is to thrive.

2

AUTHENTICITY DEFINED

"Words have meaning and names have power."

—AUTHOR UNKNOWN

A LESSON FROM MOM

It's parent/teacher night, and Mom and I enter my elementary school just as things get underway. Although I'm an excellent student and well-behaved, by the time we visit with my third teacher, I realize I'm in trouble. Mom overlooked her concern twice but isn't willing to do it a third time.

My teachers are calling me Natasha, pronounced NA-TAWSH-A. Think TAWSH rhymes with POSH, which is how it's typically pronounced by like 99.9 percent of people in the world named Natasha. However, Mom chose something different. My name is pronounced NA-TASH-A (rhymes with CASH). Family and friends call me Tash.

After she hears "NATAWSHA" for the third time, Mom's neck spins toward me. "Why are your teachers calling you that?" I say it doesn't really matter to me, which leads to a look on Mom's face conveying it's best to shut my mouth. She turns back to my teacher, tells her how to pronounce my name correctly, and asks her to share it with the other teachers so they could rectify it immediately.

Back at home, Mom shares it is unacceptable to allow people to mispronounce my name. She explains my name is an important part of my identity, and people should be respectful enough to say it correctly. She tells me it's my job to correct people, right from the start. Then Mom leans in closer to me and says, "Always insist people get your name right. It's who you are, Natasha." I didn't understand before, but I get it now. The next day, I begin correcting teachers and classmates alike. When they get it right, it makes me smile because, after all, it's who I am and I'm proud of it.

As I think of it now, my name is my identity. It makes me unique. Only once in my lifetime have I come across another person who pronounces her name like I do. Mom didn't want me to be thought of as anyone else who spells their name just like mine. She wanted people to hear my name and think of the unique woman I am. I have established my personal brand—a connecter who is authentic, caring, compassionate and principled, and my brand goes with my name. Don't let nobody call you a name you don't want to answer to!

WHAT EXACTLY IS AUTHENTICITY?

Merriam-Webster.com defines authentic this way: true to one's own personality, spirit, or character. When I think of authenticity I remember the saying "some people talk the talk but don't walk the walk." I was one of them. I'd say things I thought others wanted to hear even when it differed from how I truly felt. Once I stopped uttering words not true to myself, I learned what freedom feels like.

Here's how some of the individuals I interviewed for *Fiercely Joyful* define it:

"The very first thing that came to mind is when your walk and talk match. It's truly that simple. And if my walk and talk don't match, it really bothers me. Or if somebody else's doesn't match, I notice it right away."

—TAMARA CHRISTIAN

Yeeeessssss! It's like a Spidey-Sense in my spine. I, too, physically feel it when someone isn't being authentic.

"To me, it means just being me. When I approach a situation, I remind myself that it's okay to be me. I don't need to be ashamed about it. I don't need to apologize for it. I love me for who I am."

—DEMETRE DOWNING

Downing's description is straightforward and powerful. It's okay to care about what others think of you except when it's at your detriment. No shame or embarrassment—instead, self-love.

"It's living in a way that's true to your values and that doesn't sacrifice your needs, wants, dreams, or desires as a human. It's when you live authentically, you stop self-abandoning. I feel like those are really an antithesis of each other. You can't be authentic to yourself and your values if you self-abandon."
—CATHY KADING

Kading hits on something I'm not surprised I learned while writing *Fiercely Joyful*, though it disappoints me. So many men and women I talked to admitted to self-abandoning on a consistent basis. Folks are disregarding their own feelings in favor of what others want. This is a challenge we're going to face together, y'all.

"It means being true to who I am, being true to what I believe, being true to the things that are important to me and also using my voice. It's being true to who I am without apology."
—ALYCE HOOD

"Living authentically to me means living the life you want to live and not what others want you to or think you should live. It means not really caring what others think of you or what you are doing. It feels liberating when you realize that you don't need to live up to others' expectations of you. You realize

how much power that you give others when you worry about
their opinions or expectations of you."

—DR. MARISOL CRAIG

WHY AUTHENTICITY MATTERS

I've learned through my own experiences being authentic is the foundation of curating the life you love. Being true to yourself drives fulfillment, peace with self, happiness, meaningful relationships, confidence, and enduring joy. Your authentic self is what makes you unique. I believe the universe or God made you with purpose. You've got a job to do on this Earth. You've got a mark to make. That only happens in the way it's meant to when you are true to yourself.

In *The Gifts of Imperfection: 10th Anniversary Edition*, Brené Brown writes, "Authenticity is a collection of choices that we have to make every day. It's about the choice to show up and be real. The choice to be honest. The choice to let our true selves be seen" (2020, 67).

I love Brown's quote above—"a collection of choices" resonates with me (Brown, 2020, 67). For too long I convinced myself I *had* to do certain things to have the life I wanted. There are obvious exceptions. If you want to be a physician, you have to go to medical school. On the other hand, I didn't *have to* put on a full face of makeup and chemically straighten my hair to be seen as attractive, but I chose to. It's easy for me to say now, but a couple of decades ago I was convinced I didn't have a choice. I think the reason we default to "I have no choice" is we're so uncomfortable with the anticipated consequences of choosing differently, we behave like it's not an option. There are times when we grapple with the idea of an unfavorable outcome we can't stomach and so we say, "I had to."

All right y'all, let's put the stinky fish on the table: Choosing authenticity is *hard*. Why? Because everywhere we look, on TV, social media, perusing websites, society is trying to convince us to be someone or something we're not. Maybe it's being a successful entrepreneur. Perhaps a perfect parent with perfect children. Earning an Ivy League degree. A person who looks flawless everywhere they go. A world traveler. Fit and trim because you eat well and never miss a workout. Happy all the time, never having a bad day. Always in control and brimming with confidence. Someone with a balanced life who can do it all—successful at work, home, and a pillar in the community. Welp, that's a facade. You wouldn't necessarily know it from the advertisements flooding the airways and internet, but we all know life isn't perfect. If anyone tells you theirs is, maybe they just haven't gotten around to admitting the truth to themselves yet.

I love my life and have for about a decade now. It's not a perfect life. I'm not rich, I'm overweight, my parents and both sets of grandparents passed away many years ago, I've survived physical abuse and rape, I've battled anxiety and depression for years, and I'm a Black woman in America. I could allow those things and others to bring me down. Instead, I've made a different choice—or maybe a collection of them, like Brené Brown says in the quote above—to focus on what I love about my life and also acknowledge what I don't. I am abundantly blessed. As I write, I sit next to the window feeling sunshine warm my face. I take a moment to close my eyes and be present so I can remember that feeling when I'm having a tough day.

Making the choice to embrace joy didn't come easy. No one told me what I'm going to tell you. Perhaps I would have made healthier choices sooner. Thank goodness it's never too late to make a different choice—one leading to a fulfilling and joyful life. And guess what? Once you've chosen joy for yourself, no one can take it away. No one. Folks might try because they envy your joy. What I want you to acknowledge right here and now is someone can only take away your joy if you *allow* them to. Yep, another choice you get to make. And even when it's hard as hell to do it, I'm going to give you the tools to choose *you*.

AM I NAKED?

It's gonna feel like you're naked when you start peeling off layers to show who you really are under your armor. It keeps us feeling protected, like no one can hurt us as long as we've got a barrier between them and us. Hmm... sounds logical, but is it actually true? Can you honestly say you never experienced hurt when you were walking around all suited up? I can't. When I was busy hiding me, it chipped away at my soul because I was living a life to please others. I couldn't find joy there. Happiness at times, yes, but fleeting. Never enduring or Fierce Joy. So yes, expect to feel vulnerable (I'll help you learn how in

Chapter 3). It will be uncomfortable at first, but I know for sure that it feels much better than being in hiding.

FITTING IN

"*Authenticity is when you can be exactly who you are, all the experiences and things that shape you, and then bring that to the table in a way that isn't trying to be like anybody but yourself. It's showing up as you and not feeling like you have to put on a certain face or take off a certain face either. That is the core of what being authentic means.*"

—MELISSA PROCTOR, AUTHOR AND
CMO, ATLANTA HAWKS

After reading her book, *From Ball Girl to CMO*, I knew I had to talk to Melissa Proctor about her journey in authenticity. As a child of West Indian parents growing up in Miami, Proctor remembers not fitting in so easily. Very similar to my own childhood, she used an analogy familiar in the Black community of being an Oreo—black on the outside and white on the inside. It's frustrating but not uncommon for Black people to be labeled by other Black people for "acting White" because we're studious, don't use slang, or are perceived to like things not typically of interest in the Black community (heavy metal music is an example).

"I was always the quirky art girl who didn't fit into any crew," Proctor shared. Although it was a challenging time for her as a kid, she now sees it as "probably the biggest blessing of my life because it made me and shaped me into who I am today." She didn't hear the word "authenticity" much when she was growing up, but her mom demonstrated it every day. Proctor's mom was "so unabashedly herself" in any context.

Proctor continued to find herself in spaces where she stood out as different. She went to Wake Forest University, where her classmates told her she belonged at NYU or some other big-city school. Even though she had very different lived experiences from her fellow students, she enjoyed Wake Forest. There, Proctor learned how to interact with different types of people. She then landed in corporate America at TNT, a cable television network, where she didn't know anyone and few colleagues were as young as her. Something felt different there. In spaces with other creatives in her personal life, everybody showed up as their true selves—from dancers to designers to artists, everyone was who they were. In the corporate world, it was rigid and structured, even in her creative work environment, so she felt like she had to assimilate. She started adjusting her behavior and how she engaged so she could fit in.

The changes in how she was showing up didn't go unnoticed. Proctor recounted what the then president of TNT explained. "He said your history, your experiences, your cultural heritage are why you're here, and you would do our company a disservice by trying to put that away to be more like the masses when the reality is we brought you here because of all those differences." She shared, "That taught me what authenticity is." Wow... I *love* what the TNT president said to Proctor. That's the type of leadership under which I can thrive. I give similar counsel to my colleagues, whether peers, superiors, or subordinates. Without a doubt, we get the best outcomes when folks bring their whole perspectives to the table, and if I sense that someone is biting their tongue, I make space for their input by inviting their opinion.

I asked Proctor whether her relationships played a role in how she showed up. As she reflected on it, she shared that relationships are important, and at work it could be management or peers providing support. A junior colleague, one of a few minorities, mentioned that when she took vacations, she shifted to a protective and convenient hairstyle like braids but removed them before returning to work. Based on general conversations with her colleagues, she believed braids would garner negative attention. Proctor suggested she try keeping her braids once to see what happened. I appreciate Proctor offering advice because this is an example of how we make assumptions that drive our behaviors rather than operating on facts.

After a beach trip, Proctor's coworker returned to work with her braids for a full week. She told Proctor her colleagues loved her hair—compliments flew in! So worried about others' perceptions, she self-censored her own appearance. Talking to someone who shares some of her lived experiences opened her mind and gave her the confidence to just try. In line with this, Proctor suggests considering organizational culture when we look at job opportunities. "Whenever you interview for a job, you are interviewing them, and they are interviewing you." She firmly believes that "every culture ain't for everybody."

I'll add, pay attention to what people say *and* do. You'll see clues that inform you about the culture.

Proctor recalls a young lady who came to an interview wearing a nose ring. The candidate's current employer didn't permit nose rings, requiring her to remove it for work. When Proctor, the chief marketing officer, entered wearing a nose ring, the candidate thought to herself, *I've found my home.* The visual of an executive with a nose ring helped her see the culture at the Hawks was more aligned with who she is as a person. Proctor believes if you find yourself in an environment not welcoming you as you are, it may be time to change your environment. That's not always easy, but it is your choice.

DO YOU HAVE YOUR OWN BACK?

We all want people to show up for us. It feels good when you have a friend, colleague, or partner you know you can count on without a doubt. I remember reading in *Girl, Wash Your Face* by Rachel Hollis. We would never want to be friends with a person who doesn't show up—always late, always cancels, does things half-assed, and is essentially uncommitted to following through (2018, 22). It was a lightbulb moment for me because I never thought of it from that perspective. When I reflected on how little I was following through for *me*, I recognized that I would not want to be my friend at all.

I spoke with Sylvia Matthews, a senior vice president for a large medical supply corporation, about what authenticity means to her. Matthews has built her professional reputation on exhibiting high integrity and an unrelenting work ethic. Because she feels an overwhelming sense of responsibility to do what's right, she's well-connected to her values. "I don't know how to be any other way," she said.

When I asked about any correlation she's experienced between living authentically and experiencing joy and fulfillment in her life, Matthews expressed a great sense of fulfillment from doing everything she does for her family and at work with the highest of quality. She admits to struggling with perfection but feels good about doing her best and showing up for her loved ones. Unfortunately, she doesn't do the same for herself.

Matthews says she hasn't reached self-actualization. In other words, her personal potential remains unrealized. She's a successful, Ivy League-educated professional who also has creative talent. Unfortunately, the day-to-day life of a corporate executive, wife, and busy mom doesn't easily yield time to employ creative skills. Her best chance to unleash her creativity is when "helping" her kids with school assignments. Y'all know what I'm going to say, right? Matthews kinda sorta definitely takes over the kids' creative school projects! It's an opportunity for her to let her creative juices flow, and she absolutely loves it. It brings her joy.

One of Matthews's children has a personality very different from her own. Her youngest daughter is a "girly-girl" who loves makeup and fashion. She's got tons of flair and loves being unique. Matthews prefers a classic, more conservative style. Still, Matthews encourages her daughter to dress the way *she* wants to dress—mismatched colors and all. She bites her tongue when her daughter makes wardrobe choices Matthews would never entertain for herself because she doesn't want her daughter to feel like she has to conform to anyone else's idea of beauty. Matthews wants her to do what makes her happy. As she shares her insights, it's clear Matthews hasn't empowered herself the same way—to do what makes *her* happy.

Matthews may be dealing with a combination of fear of the unknown and guilt about the idea of focusing on herself, which prevents her from living in integrity with her own needs—those needs foundational to her joy. Being authentic for herself is taking a back seat. Matthews does show up for herself sometimes, but not in ways that bring her enduring joy. It's typically when she feels it's the right thing to do or she's made a commitment to take on a challenge with a friend, so she is driven to follow through and not let her friend down.

Folks, hear me and hear me well. It is unacceptable to show up for everyone else and not for you. Living in alignment with your values *except* when it comes to you, isn't living a fully authentic life. Not following through on your promises to yourself is *not* okay. Sure, it will happen from time to time, but we have to make it the exception, not the rule. You have a responsibility to yourself to meet your own needs physically, emotionally, mentally, and spiritually. And when you do, you show up *even better* for everyone else.

KEYS TO BEING FIERCELY JOYFUL:

What authenticity looks like for you depends on who you are. Take the important step of finding out if you don't already know. Here's how:

- **Date yourself.** You know how when you first start dating someone, you ask all kinds of questions to get to know them? Do the same and get to know you. What inspires you? What brings you joy? What zaps your energy or crushes your spirit? Do your friends *really* know you? If no, why not? Consider journaling what you learn. Take some time over a few months or so to learn about you so you can be intentional about doing what and behaving how it feeds your soul.

- **Explore your values.** You need to know your top two to three values because they will drive how you show up, what you're willing and not willing to do, how you behave, etc. It may take some time to nail down your answers. When I review a list of values (use your web browser to find one), I always resonate with fifteen to twenty. You might too, but you'll need to narrow it down. When you make decisions, you should assess what choice is in alignment with your top values—the ones you absolutely won't compromise. Keep in mind, values can change as life changes. If you've identified your values in the past, it might be great timing for a validation check.

- **Practice mindfulness.** It's important to pay attention to your own behavior so you can monitor how authentic you are or are not being. Authenticity is something you have to work at every day. There isn't a sudden arrival point. You'll find yourself slipping at times and winning at others. Accept it, monitor it, and adjust it when needed.

- 🔑 **Be courageous**. It's completely normal to feel discomfort or fear about being authentic. Start small and keep progressing over time. For example, start with not saying yes when you really want to say no. I'm sure you've heard before: no is a complete sentence. Don't feel the need to give reasons or make excuses for your no, just say it and move on. "No, I won't be at your party, Jeff. I appreciate you inviting me." If Jeff asks why, don't make something up! Simply say, "Don't worry, we'll get together soon." Then, feel free to change the subject.

3

BE VULNERABLE

Being vulnerable makes you look weak. I've heard it said many times, and I'm calling BS, y'all. It's nonsense. I'd say the erroneous belief stems from one's own fear of judgment. The willingness to be vulnerable requires courage to move beyond what others might think.

Brené Brown, author of *Daring Greatly: How the Courage to Be Vulnerable Transforms the Way We Live, Love, Parent, and Lead*, confirms in her book research we tend to celebrate vulnerability as a strength in other people, yet the same doesn't usually to apply to ourselves. "We love seeing raw truth and openness in other people, but we are afraid to let them see it in us " (2012, 41). After a speaking engagement, people often express appreciation for my openness. Next to my authenticity, my vulnerability seems to resonate with audiences most. People comment on how brave I am to be so open, which aligns with Brown's findings. "Vulnerability is courage in you and inadequacy in me" (2012, 42). Can't quite put my finger on how I became comfortable with it; however, I know my willingness to be vulnerable changed my life in the most amazing way.

So, what is vulnerability? I know for sure it's something many of us are so afraid to show that we end up burying it. The definition of vulnerable, according to Merriam-Webster.com, is: capable of being physically or emotionally wounded. Hmm... Looking at those words, I definitely see where fear might come into play. Doesn't sound inspiring.

Professionally speaking, Harvard Business Review discusses results of an online survey conducted by Harris Poll in which 69 percent of managers say they're uncomfortable communicating with employees in general, while 20 percent of respondents are specifically uncomfortable with demonstrating vulnerability (Solomon 2016). Being vulnerable is part of being authentic—we share our truth at the risk of being judged, hurt, or having it used against us. It's still our truth, and we don't control what others do with it. When we share it, though, it's the basis of the trust, which deepens relationships, bringing opportunity and growth into our lives.

There are times when we have to be vulnerable to fight for our own needs. It can be the difference between good and great. Whether we're managing our work or managing our lives, Margie Warrell says it well in her book, *Brave: 50 Everyday Acts of Courage to Thrive in Work, Love and Life.* "Every worthwhile endeavor requires making yourself vulnerable" (Warrell 2015, 35).

FROM TRAGEDY TO GROWTH

In 2020, I live and work in Atlanta while my husband is back home in the Washington, DC, metro area. Like so many Americans and people across the world, I'm filled with a spectrum of emotions... sadness, anger, disbelief, anxiety, and fear while grappling with the murder of George Floyd Jr.

Since it's early in the COVID-19 pandemic, many of us are home. I'm teleworking, fortunate enough my work can be accomplished virtually. The television is on all day long, which means I see the video of Floyd's murder again, again, and again. It's on every news channel I watch every day. Bubbling inside me is an overwhelming need to say *something*. I'm leading an organization of more than 300 employees and contractors. Not only do I know I must acknowledge it, I know it's irresponsible for me not to.

Some leaders prefer to keep work separate from the rest of our lives. The fact is, we no longer live in a world operating with such boundaries We don't compartmentalize like people did and even were expected to in years past. We are *whole* people. To pretend what happens at home or in the world around us doesn't impact us at work is a disservice to you and your colleagues. And if you're a manager like me who owns and appreciates the responsibility to support her team, the disservice is exponentially greater. Now, this doesn't mean you need a couch in your office. It means you have a responsibility to acknowledge people are more than their work.

In her book *Dare to Lead: Brave Work. Tough Conversations. Whole Hearts,* Brené Brown said, "Daring leaders who live their values are never silent about hard things" (2018, 194). I've memorized Brown's quote. It sticks with and reminds me when I need to act. I pull out my iPad, hit record, and start talking. I acknowledge the murder of George Floyd being a horrific act at the hands of police. I talk about how I feel in this moment as a Black woman: the way goosebumps cover my body and a pit forms in my stomach when I worry about my Black husband, Edwaun, being pulled over by the police.

Edwaun is soft-spoken at times, has a medium build, and dark brown skin. What if he upsets a police officer? If he doesn't seem deferential enough? If he asks questions about why he's being pulled over? If he reaches for his license and doesn't say it loudly enough for the officer to understand? I tell my colleagues it's important I acknowledge people on our team are hurting. I want to provide a safe space for us to have candid discussions about how we feel. I invite anyone who is interested to join me virtually for a lunchtime Brown Bag session I call "An Open Conversation."

When I initiate the open conversations, we're in the midst of a focused effort from the presidential administration to tamp down training related to diversity and inclusion in the federal workplace. My hand gets slapped for training planned several months before the executive order is issued. Once discovered, I'm directed to cancel it. I worry I could lose my job just for having the open conversations. Still, I knew I had to do it. I believe it irresponsible for me, a woman of color with a team of humans who have emotions just like me, to be silent.

When we convene our first Zoom conversation, I start with simple ground rules:

- Be respectful, whether you agree or not,
- Be professional,
- No use of profanity or racial slurs,
- No question is off limits,
- Anyone who wishes to can answer questions/weigh in, and;
- More than one person may weigh in, allowing for a variety of perspectives to be shared.

I kick things off by explaining the difference between being racist, nonracist, and anti-racist. I also suggest opportunities for learning—books, podcasts, TEDx Talks and more. When I invite questions, the first isn't what I expect. One colleague asks, "Should I say Black or African American? I never know what I'm supposed to say." I proceed to give the arguably least satisfying answer, "Welp, it depends."

It's the truth—how we want to be identified is based on our lived experiences. In my early twenties, I marry for the first time. My then husband is from a West African family and is their first-born American child. I learn during our marriage how much *some* Africans dislike Black Americans. Our marriage ends in divorce less than two years later, partially because of the trauma I experience in how he allows his family to treat me. My invisible scars leave me with absolutely no desire to be called any name referencing Africa. Might sound harsh; nevertheless, I'm entitled to my preference. I was born in America. I am a Black woman. Please refer to me as such. Thank you kindly.

On the other hand, calling a person Black may elicit a visceral reaction if they were raised to know themselves not as a color—often used with negative connotations like blacklist, blackball, and black mark, to name a few—but as an ancestor from a people who were stolen from their homes, brought to America enslaved, and not only survived unspeakable horrors, they eventually thrived. See the different perspectives? No BIPOC (Black, Indigenous, and People of Color) population is a monolith. I tell my colleagues what goes for one does *not* go for all. We can't assume, we have to ask. Let us all respect people enough to ask their preference and then follow through.

Many more questions follow. Perspectives and experiences are shared. "Thank you so much for joining our Open Conversation. I learned from all I heard, and I hope you did too. Let me ask your thoughts; should we do this again?" The number of thumbs-up emojis, shaking heads, and "yes" in the chat tells me the conversations are needed. By the time we have our third Open Conversation, more people are actively participating in the discussion and even turning on their cameras. Seeing vulnerability in action inspires.

VULNERABILITY IS HARD

Like anything else, it gets easier the more often you do it. I gain insights from a leader and mentor, Jeffrey Planty, who is the recipient of the 2022 Presidential Rank Award, one of the most prestigious awards in federal career civil service. Planty, a senior executive, says, "When you're not vulnerable, when you're afraid to admit you're wrong or you have a weakness, you're not living into your best self. It's core to your authenticity. You have to be empathetic, and you have to be vulnerable." Planty believes there is a payoff you get from allowing yourself to be vulnerable. "Acts of vulnerability will win you the reputation of being an authentic person and not being afraid of championing an opposing view."

In one example, it seems one of my peers is never satisfied with the work of me and my team. He frequently shares complaints and criticisms. My perception of his dissatisfaction makes me study our engagement through a lens inevitably influenced by my personal beliefs. I realize I need to address it because holding it in isn't serving either of us well. "I'm sensing my team, and I aren't meeting your needs. We're trying, yet it seems we're missing the mark. Will you share with me your feedback? What concerns you, and what can we do to provide the support you need?"

"I wasn't aware you felt this way. That's actually not true at all. I'm very satisfied with the service you're delivering." He goes on to explain he's very analytical and constantly seeks ways to improve. What I see as criticism is his way of trying to increase or maximize efficiencies.

Plus, he's not one who calls attention to what's going well unless it's something extraordinary. Our conversation gives me clarity about what drives him and helps him see an opportunity to balance feedback on where we can improve with express acknowledgment of a job well done. Putting my ego aside and seeking feedback moves me toward resolution.

When discussing what it takes to be authentic with a colleague, she shared, "I don't need courage. I need to be vulnerable. I like to say all the time, the universe is rigged in my favor. And whatever's going to happen is going to happen. So I just need to be vulnerable to that. And the funny thing about vulnerability is the more I talk about the underbelly, the easier it becomes." The underbelly—those unpleasant or hard things we shouldn't shy away from. The underbelly is where we see the potential for risk but do what scares us anyway.

WHY BEING VULNERABLE MATTERS

When I think about how I contribute to the world around me, I'm proud of the Open Conversations and other similar discussions I facilitate. Even if only one person's perspective is broadened, my actions make a difference. The outcomes of not shying away from hard things include building trust as a team, modeling behavior I wish for others to follow, demonstrating how to talk about difficult topics, and creating space for curiosity, understanding, and growth. More importantly, the group of us develop a greater willingness to reflect on another person's truth.

The engagement from my team inspires and motivates me to continue helping others learn how to have candid discussions productively and embrace healthy conflict. It emboldens me too. I lean in more, unwilling to shy away from the hard stuff. Before I realize it, it becomes part of my personal brand. My colleagues recognize they can depend on me to call things out, hold myself and others accountable and, as we often say in my workplace, "put the stinky fish on the table" professionally and effectively. My efforts garner respect from my team, colleagues, and senior management, now expecting me to use my voice for myself and others.

We can't be fully authentic without being vulnerable. For me, it comes naturally now, and it's rarely uncomfortable. When I need to do or say hard things with potential to hurt or upset others, I encounter discomfort. However, the misalignment or guilt I'll feel if I *don't* act is much worse. At this stage in my life, I'm an open book. I believe the universe helps us through the most difficult challenges of life to allow us to be of service to others who face similar experiences, which is why I tell all. If I can help just one person see they can persevere, I'm grateful, and it's worth it. I also find it therapeutic to say some things out loud... just acknowledge them out in the ether. It's freeing.

In Dr. Margie Warrell's article, "Be Brave: Why You Need to Risk Vulnerability to Build Great Relationships" she offers, "Our lives expand in proportion to the quality of our relationships, and the quality of our relationships expand with our willingness to get comfortable feeling uncomfortable" (Warrell 2018). The quality of my relationships today is immeasurably greater than when I didn't embrace and present my whole self. I'm energized by the deep connections I have and continue to build with others.

Countless blessings come to me because I own and speak my truth. I'm often amazed at the support, connections, opportunities, and learning I've gained from empowering myself to be myself. I'll come home and tell my husband I was asked to be a keynote speaker, invited to appear on a podcast, or a new contact offers to host a book party for *Fiercely Joyful*. "Honey, I can't believe it! I met her three weeks ago, and she's willing to support me in this way? Just wow!" Edwaun lets me get all my giddiness out and nods. "Well, congratulations. I'm not surprised at all. People gravitate toward you and believe in what you have to say."

His inside voice response is more like *I don't know why these things surprise you… they happen all the time.* One of my good friends says, "He saw in you from the beginning what you're only recognizing now. Edwaun saw your potential right from the start." I believe having no expectation of such blessings to come my way is what inspires me to celebrate each one like the first. Now it's your turn. Open up, push through the discomfort, and realize the benefits of being vulnerable.

Here's what embracing vulnerability looks like in practice:

- **Accept that this feels scary and push past it.** Being vulnerable is being outside your comfort zone. If you're connected with your gut, you'll feel it when you're there. Experiencing fear of judgment or consequence is not uncommon. Remind yourself of this beforehand, and then put yourself out there anyway.
- **Let down your walls, not necessarily your guard.** There's a way to be vulnerable *and* look out for yourself. You assess your environment while you're being vulnerable. Watch body language, eye contact, and engagement from your audience. Adjust as you sense you need to.
- **When you don't know the answer, say so.** Whether it's something said in a meeting, a question your manager asks you, or a reference your new acquaintance makes, be willing to say, "I don't know."
- **Be forthcoming with others about your mistakes.** Proactively own your missteps and make a point of sharing it with others who can learn from your experience.
- **Don't accept the myth that vulnerability is a sign of weakness.** You know who came up with that? Folks who envy those who demonstrate both vulnerability and strength... hmph. I refuse to accept that premise because I have a career full of experiences that have shown me just the opposite. Be courageous and show what you authentically feel. It's worth it.

4

GET CONNECTED

"Instinct is a marvelous thing. It can neither be explained nor ignored."

—AGATHA CHRISTIE

A LESSON FROM MOM

Mom believes firmly in God. We attend Bethel AME (African Methodist Episcopal) church every Sunday. We're both in the choir, and Mom has been the church treasurer for several years. Her dedication to the church and all the people in it is extraordinary. She volunteers to help with every event and activity, from bringing cakes for a bake sale to setting up the basement for a fish fry to planning the annual church bazaar.

Every night, Mom gets on her knees, leans on the side of her bed, and bows her head in silent prayer. I do the same, except I say the same kid's prayer each time: *Now I lay me down to sleep, I pray the Lord my soul to keep. If I should die before I wake, I pray the Lord my soul to take.*

It's Mom's unwavering commitment to her faith keeping her connected to what's happening on the inside, in her spirit. As for me, I'm more spiritual than religious at this point in my life. Perhaps you're neither, which is just fine. How you get connected doesn't matter as much as doing it. I'll share my unusual journey, and you'll see the answer to *how* is up to you.

~————————

The first time I sense death coming, it's scary and heartbreaking. I want absolutely nothing to do with what I feel and decide right then and there, I'm going to ignore it. I pretend it didn't happen, tell no one, and move on.

It's April 1, 1990, my sweet sixteenth birthday. Mom plans a big party for me, and I'm excited to celebrate with my friends and family. There's a table in the corner overflowing with gifts I can't wait to open. We dance the night away, and I feel like the most special girl in the world!

After cleaning up, I go to Nana's room to wish her goodnight. My grandmother is stricken with lung cancer and a brain tumor. She moves in with us as the cancer takes a toll on her body, and she's no longer able to care for herself. Nana takes my room; it's the warmest in the house, and she's always cold. I smile when she sleeps soundly in the twin-sized canopy bed I love so much. Terminally ill,

Nana is weak and no longer eating or speaking, so she didn't join the party. She looks me in my eyes, and I lean in to kiss her. She places her hand on my cheek. Her lips curve, revealing the slightest smile, which felt like the best birthday gift ever. I snuggle under my own covers still giddy, falling asleep replaying the wonderful night in my mind.

When I wake, around three a.m., I hear Mom sobbing down the hall. My body is overcome with fear and dread because I know what's happening. It came to me after I got home from school two days earlier. It was a little voice inside telling me Nana is ready to go to heaven.

I jump out of bed and run to Nana's room. When I touch her, she's so cold. Tears flowing and hugging Mom, I'm angry the little voice was right. Even though Nana was suffering, it's so hard to lose her. I never gave up hope she would get better, praying for it every night before bed. In time, I remember feeling humbled by Nana waiting to surrender until after my special day. Her kindness and compassion remained until the very end.

Next time I hear the voice, it's nearly five years later on February 11, 1995, when Mom is suffering from her worst cancer relapse yet. Still in bed, I open my eyes and hear the little voice telling me Mom is on the verge of taking her last breath. I can't bear to be home when it happens, so I quickly get dressed and leave after kissing Mom goodbye. I'm pacing up and down grocery store aisles when the call comes. Mom is gone.

The little voice visits me several more times, each instance ahead of someone's death. It's not limited to my loved ones anymore. Out of the blue, I hear it telling me someone is going to perish, and it's *never* wrong. *I don't want a special sense about death. Why me and what am I supposed to do with the information when it comes?* Finally, I stop trying to ignore it. It's my turn to surrender and let my spirit communicate with me. Once I welcome the little voice, my first message about something *good* is delivered.

PREMONITIONS

Before I intentionally connect with my intuition, I get premonitions—a strong feeling something is about to happen—about all kinds of things and seemingly with no rhyme or reason. The little voice is sharing with me something is about to happen. It feels as if I'm making up for lost time when the premonitions come more frequently. I realize, though, it's like when you buy a car: suddenly you see the same make and model much more often. Everyone didn't go out and buy a two-door hardtop cream-colored Mini Cooper the same week I did. Instead, I'm simply paying closer attention and noticing what's been there all along.

You know how someone crosses your mind randomly, and you're not sure why? It happens to me often. I've learned, for me, it's an intentional prompt to connect with them. I follow through, and the reason for the prompt is revealed to me. Sometimes it's someone I don't know well at all, perhaps a colleague. The last time it happened after a meeting with a coworker I hadn't seen in months. Something about her energy doesn't seem right. A couple of weeks later, she pops back into my mind, so I text asking her to let me know when she can chat.

When we connect, I tell her she might think I'm crazy (upfront disclaimer!), yet I felt an urge to reach out to her. "Last time I saw you, it seemed like you had a lot of weight on your shoulders. Is there any support I can offer?" She's stunned and tearing up. I acknowledge we don't know each other well (and my intention isn't to get all up in her business); still, I want to support her and make sure she's okay. Although things are great personally, she confesses, "I'm dealing with some struggles at work, and would like to get some advice when I get back in town." She later texts, "Thank you so much! You warmed my heart!" I'm happy I followed through because now she knows someone at work (me) cares about her as a human being. "You have no idea how much you've helped me by just picking up the phone." In those times when we feel lonely at work, it's such a relief to learn we're not really alone at all.

For those of you driven by having answers, structure, and clarity, getting connected to your intuition will be a bit tougher for you, though not impossible. I mentioned it took me years to stop ignoring mine, and I know now it wasn't just the worry about knowing something bad was coming before it happened. It was also the discomfort of not fully understanding the message, yet knowing I need to acknowledge and act on it anyway. I've since grown comfortable with the lack of clarity—I accept it as an exercise in patience and surrender to the universe.

In early 2022, I have a strong intuition about the rest of the year ahead. It's incredibly positive, and a seed is planted around remarkable experiences to come. It's intriguing knowing goodness is in store, so I navigate through most of my days with a sense of anticipation and excitement, being purposeful in following through on the commitments I make to myself and others. Here is some of what happened:

- After enrolling in a group writing program called Modern Authors by Book Creators, I publish my first book (yes, the one you're reading!) after years of dreaming, not doing.
- I'm selected for a permanent appointment as a vice president overseeing day-to-day operations for a critical support organization of more than 1,500 federal and contract human resources.
- I'm invited to join a powerful women's networking organization, broadening my network and opening doors to amazing opportunities.
- I show up as me, authentically, wherever I am and whomever I'm with. Sometimes, being authentic means being silent. Showing up as I want to becomes nonnegotiable and serves my spirit well.

These are just a few highlights—there is so much more. Countless moments of happiness, no shortage of excitement, learning all along the way, and plenty of joy... It's a fantastic year on purpose. I'd be remiss not to mention I know my positive attitude helped draw in goodness in my life. Our mindset is powerful and can influence outcomes. To learn more about my experiences and perspectives, read on to Chapter 8: Be Grateful.

I'm calling attention to premonitions because I've encountered a number of people choosing to ignore them as I did. I believe we sometimes dismiss what we don't understand. Although I wish I could connect to premonition on demand, it comes when it comes. The discomfort and fear I felt led me to shake them off. Now, I treasure premonitions—both good and bad. If bad, I facilitate engagement. For example, if I have a premonition about death, I connect with the person if they're in my circle, and encourage others to do the same. If it's about sickness, I'll encourage a doctor's visit. If any of what I describe sounds like an experience you've had, consider tuning in to your premonitions. Premonitions can be helpful if we're willing to hear/see them, which requires us to get connected to ourselves.

CONNECTING TO INTUITION GROUNDS YOU

We often think about intuition in terms of our gut feelings or a hunch. It's tough to accept at first because we have no explanation for why we suddenly have complete knowing of something. Merriam-Webster.com defines it as: the power or faculty of attaining to direct knowledge or cognition without evident rational thought and inference. Hmm... a definition instilling confidence we should follow intuitions? *Not*. Thinking of it as our personal compass or North Star helps. I lean into my intuition often, using it to help me make decisions, especially those with risk involved.

Reggie Hubbard, chief serving officer of Active Peace Yoga in the Washington, DC, area was raised by strong Black women grounded in their faith and ancestry. Hubbard's mother and grandmother instilled in him the fullest awareness of how he should be treated. His experiences learning from them reminds me of a quote I love from Moïra Fowley-Doyle's book *Spellbook of the Lost and Found*, "Do no harm but take no shit" (Fowley-Doyle 2017, 3). *Love!*

"You cannot have impact if you don't have acquaintance with self." Hubbard says this applies to impact on self, others, and the world around you. He leverages self-connectedness to prepare for important life experiences by checking in with himself to confirm his readiness. "I refuse to enter a situation when I'm not resourced, meaning, if I don't have enough energy to be in a situation, I won't go into the situation. And that's important. We often exhaust ourselves or are unaware of our exhaustion. The first key to instinct is awareness of the physical body."

As a teacher, Hubbard seeks to awaken his student's intuition. He sees connection between mind and body as something essential and liberating in his life. It might be his inner voice telling him to call someone he hasn't talked to in years or something more substantive like seeking a new career path. "These things can't come through if you haven't created space for them to manifest."

Hubbard says the more you practice, the deeper the connectedness you'll experience.

How many times have you shrugged off those feelings? If you're like most people, including me, more times than you can count. Like the time you knew you weren't in the right mental space for a tough conversation when you got home after a tough workday. Or maybe it's Thanksgiving dinner with the fam who knows you're nonbinary yet continues to call you "he/him." For me, times when I push myself to do something out of sync with my emotional, mental, or physical state chip away at me. I leave a part of me behind to make someone else feel good. What good comes to me as a result? Nada. So let's not keep doing what we know ain't right.

Hubbard told me he was angry. His anger manifested in the day-to-day struggles of being a Black man in America. He even suffered from stress-induced eczema, which scarred his body. One day, a friend invited him to join her for yoga, and his curiosity made him go. He tried it yet didn't see a place for himself—an overweight Black man in his forties. I couldn't agree more because I've "tried" yoga about half a dozen times, and I'm usually the only way overweight person in the room, typically the only person of color, and older than most. So yeah, like Hubbard, I didn't feel like I fit in. Thankfully, he stuck with it because yoga has changed his life.

In time, Hubbard recognized. "You don't have to be angry unless you choose to be." Yes, I agree, it's a choice. Yoga helped him connect with himself, enabling him to transform his life. He no longer moves through the world grounded in anger. Instead, he takes the energy once manifested as constant anger and "transmutes that through yoga practice to joy. And rather than be angry all the time, I can be defiant through my joy. So defiance came as a maturation of trying to deconstruct myself from anger as my native tongue." Hubbard learned how to navigate adversity with grace. The spiritual practice of yoga taught him to exert power over his choices with intention. "I try not to do harm. And you won't take my peace. You won't take my joy."

Hubbard's take on joyful defiance moves me. I see it as yet another path to being fiercely joyful. Being connected with ourselves empowers us to find joy even in the darkest of times. It helps us summon the resiliency to be defiant in resisting being pulled into despair. In remarks titled "Joyful Defiance In the Call For Courageous Action" delivered during the Upaya Zen Center Election Series in October 2020, Hubbard shares, "Joyful defiance begins with a willingness to call things as you see it. And if done from a place of compassion and an orientation of service, it compels you to do something once you see the truth" (Hubbard 2020). This is calling a thing a thing with good intention driving the callout.

Allow me to be abundantly clear: getting connected with ourselves is *useless* if we don't follow through on what we hear, feel, and learn. Joyful defiance? It requires action. This is a must, not an option. I spent many years having premonitions and intuitions I ignored. Imagine how much sooner I could have had greater fulfillment if I wasn't so afraid to *listen to me*. Y'all, I'm being vulnerable, putting my business in the streets so you don't make my mistakes. Fear is strong and sometimes paralyzing. The longer we sit in it, the harder it is to exit, making it challenging for us to get out of our own way. However, challenging doesn't mean impossible. We can do this. The reason we have to? Following through—*listening and acting*—is a key to curating a fiercely joyful life.

BUT WAITAMINUTE...
Follow. Act. Do. But *not* blindly.

It's absolutely possible for us to influence our intuition with our emotions or our own bias—whether conscious or subconscious. We need to check ourselves to learn the difference.

When I think about the times my instinct turned out to be wrong, I was second-guessing myself or letting emotions rather than my spirit be my guide. How do you know when you're veering down the wrong road? When I'm in tune with my instincts, I feel a sense of calm and peace. You will find a stillness, a feeling of knowing and even confidence in your thoughts. And it's pretty instantaneous. If it's your intuition, it's not going to take you hours or days to get to an answer. You'll know immediately.

For me, it feels like there's a pit in my stomach, queasiness, or a feeling of unease. My body feels it when my spirit or the universe is telling me I'm about to take a wrong turn.

I allow it to help me reset. In other cases, I feel it when I've already made the wrong decision. It's still valuable even then because then I can be proactive about fixing what's gone awry.

I remember putting my foot in my mouth in a big meeting. Even though I'm known for saying things no one else wants to say, I *do* have some limits y'all! However, that time, I failed to stop and think before doing. Just ran on out into the middle of the street without looking, as if I had the right of way—not ideal.

Jot down a few of those times when you took an approach other than what you preferred as a means of compromise. What was the outcome? In my case, it was fine! Compromise is part of life and often the right thing to do. What's important is the compromise must not undermine your values. Not okay. If you feel your inner voice giving you some side-eye, you know you're on the verge of making a decision unlikely to serve you well.

KEYS TO BEING FIERCELY JOYFUL:
Try at least one of these tools, and if you're already doing one or more of them, push yourself to try something new!

- **Trust your instincts.** Sometimes, you're not going to agree with your instinct. You have to learn to trust it, which means pushing past the fear. Now, I'm not gonna tell you the fear will go away. It will come and go. What's important is to acknowledge it, allow yourself to feel it, and know you can overcome it if you *choose* to. The same applies to anything you fear.

🔑 **Embrace mindfulness.** Being mindful means being present. It means paying attention. So often, we're focusing on what comes next, and we miss what's happening right now. Instead, focus on awareness of yourself and others. How are you feeling emotionally in the moment? How are others receiving your message? How does your body feel? Use what you learn to inform what you do.

🔑 **Meditate.** Are you thinking, "Yeah... tried it. Didn't work for me"? If it's been a while, try again (I gave up *many* times before it stuck). Did you know you can do walking meditations (eyes *open*, of course!)? Meditate lying in bed before you get up? No need to sit on a pillow in a quarter-lotus position saying, "ummm." Meditating helps me focus, relieve stress, and embrace calm. Try an app or a beginner's video and meditate for five minutes daily for a week. If you don't find it's beneficial, move on!

🔑 **Journal.** What and how often you journal is up to you. And you don't have to fill an entire page. You might have two sentences one day and two paragraphs the next. I write about what I'm grateful for, adding the *Five Minute Journal* to my morning routine. It has simple morning and evening prompts to help center me when the day begins and encourage reflection on how it went.

🔑 **Be still.** This is challenging for me because the idea of sitting and quietly reflecting feels "unproductive" due to the hustle culture tendencies I'm slowly shedding.

Still, when I muster the patience to do it, the result is peacefulness. Sit on a bench outside or on the grass at a park with a cup of coffee or tea and listen to the noises around you. If you've got active kids, do this while waiting for practice to finish. Still your mind and simply be present.

5

IT'S NOT ALL
ABOUT YOU

When you speak up or show up authentically, you create room for others to follow suit. When the cold shoulder fashion trend hits retail stores, I'm all in. I love it and buy a couple of dresses sporting the shoulder cutouts. Convinced the look isn't work appropriate, I save my dresses for weekends. Then, one summer day, the chief operating officer (COO) of my organization comes into a meeting with her shoulders out! I was like... *what*? That's *allowed*? I take my cue from her and wear a cold shoulder top to work the very next day. She set the standard. Now I'm comfortable with it.

See where I'm going here? Even when you're not setting out with the intention to create space for others, it happens anyway. When you show up authentically, you give others permission to do the same. I can guarantee my former COO doesn't recall the first time she wore a cold-shoulder dress. She isn't setting out to give me permission to rock my cold shoulders. Yet, years later, I recall it like it happened yesterday. She simply shows up the way she wants to, and here I am, still aware of what I derived from the moment. What I learn is you being you is a service to *both* yourself and others. It's one of those ways you can give to others something intangible yet incredibly powerful and meaningful.

"I cannot do all the good that the world needs. But the world needs all the good that I can do."

—JANA STANFIELD

MAKE PLENTY OF SPACE

Ever been judged because you weren't conforming? Maybe you dress in a style atypical for your office or wear a headwrap. Perhaps, like me, you like bright colors, big accessories, and funky eyeglasses. The first time I wear a pair to work, my manager says, "They're a bit much—look for some more classic options!" Yes, I look at her with my eyes over the top of my glasses shaking my head as she walks out of my office. I don't respond. I don't know what to say. What I do recognize is she will consider me being "a bit much" each time I wear those glasses. It stings… I invested quite a few coins in my new frames, but in the drawer they go. My manager gets what she wants—a toned-down version of me—and I make the choice to conform.

My example is small but mighty. Is it a huge deal for me to wear other glasses to work? No, I own multiple pairs. Still, my manager's comment made me assess my *entire* work wardrobe under her assertion—what clothes or other accessories am I wearing that she considers a bit too much? My choice to conform comes from a desire to be heard and seen as a professional who is a significant contributor to the success of our organization. I don't want anything to distract from the value I provide. I make adjustments and keep it moving. At times, we prefer the safe option. What's unfortunate is my choice means I'm not creating space for the person who prefers their funky glasses.

Now, let's fast forward about six or seven years to a similar moment. I'm working in Atlanta, and one of the leaders in my organization is in town meeting with my team. The first day I see him, we greet, exchange pleasantries, and go on about the day. The next morning, he greets me saying, "Now I like your hair like *that*, Tash." I'm sporting a fresh blowout, meaning my hair is pin straight and swinging, full of body and shine. The previous day, I wore my normal "big hair, don't care" style, which is my naturally curly hair presented as it grows from my head. He didn't compliment me on my curly style—in fact, he didn't say anything about it at all.

As a Black woman, I receive his compliment as *I like when your hair looks like what I (and much of society) sees as beautiful—hair resembling a White woman's hair.* He probably isn't thinking this consciously. Instead, years of stereotyping what is and isn't attractive influences our judgment. I go home and wash the straightness out of my hair as fast as I can, pressed to show up at work curly again. The leader won't be there to see it, but it doesn't matter. What does matter is I'm showing up as me and not worried about what anyone else thinks of it. Whether curly, straight, braided, or twisted, my hair is always neat and professional, which is the only standard I should need to meet. This time, I make space for myself and others and am comfortable in doing so. Please don't wait like I did. Do you *from the start*, and then it doesn't become "a thing" when you suddenly decide to be happily nappy or whatever else you choose to do.

The simple act of taking a calculated risk liberates you and others. I wish I experienced a moment early in my career when someone who looked like me showed up at work with her hair styled the way it grows out of her head. Maybe then my own hair journey wouldn't have been so challenging. Because someone would have come before me, cracking open the door for me to enter too. As more enter, the door goes from ajar to wide open. The bottom line? Someone has to start. Why not you?

WE MAKE A MARK EVEN WHEN WE DON'T PLAN TO

We have great neighbors where we live and really enjoy getting to know them. Some folks have get-togethers in the building now and then. My husband and I are invited to one of those social events, which is a discussion based on *Truthing Cards: Questions for the Black Community to Ignite Engaging Conversations*. The card deck is designed by Randi B., a diversity and inclusion strategist and author of *Truthing: A Collection of Essays*.

I love engaging in intellectually stimulating conversations, all driven by thoughtful questions on each card. At one point, I mention I'm writing a book, though I'm not trying to promote it. I'm sharing how much reflection has come from the process. I never expect it, but find the work cathartic.

During an intermission (the event was being recorded for promotional use later), I have an opportunity for a more intimate conversation with two other participants. They ask what my book is about, and in my mind, I've been given an open invitation to not only answer their question but start offering unsolicited counsel about things I'd heard them say. Can't help myself, y'all! I struggle to turn away from a moment to help others. Who knows how it might lift them up or give them something new to consider? I *choose* to do it!

One woman talks about the reins of conformity around her at work. Her anguish in not being able to show up authentically is clear. Many of us have been there at one time or another, or maybe we're still there. The unwritten requirement to conform neutralizes us, and we believe we have no choice but to line up and salute. I tell her she has more power than she's allowing herself to use.

You can probably imagine her initial response of side-eye mixed with curiosity. She was probably thinking, *Easy for you to say because you work where they let you be you.* She's correct, although it's true because, in my case, someone else *did* crack the door open for me and others to come after her.

My point is that I don't want her to assume and focus on her limitations off the bat. Instead, we must look for the opportunities we *do have* to influence change. She is a seasoned and highly respected professional. If someone is going to be *the one* to start testing the limits, she's the best candidate. She's the one who can get away with pushing the envelope, not a brand new junior employee who us old heads might be dismissive of. Her pushing past the status quo not only creates space for her to be more authentic but also for everyone else around her to do so. I believe we have a responsibility to make space. Yes, I said *responsibility*. Because it's not all about you or me, it's about us.

I don't ever want to be the person who has "arrived" at their desired station in life yet doesn't turn around to hold out a hand for others to come with. Honestly, I can't possibly count how many hands have been extended to me over my lifetime. I am grateful for every single one. It is my responsibility, *our* responsibility, to pay forward our blessings. When it comes to living authentically, one of the best ways to repay our debt is by making space for others. Let's dig a little bit more into what making space means.

Grab your notebook and jot down your thoughts on this question: How does being true to yourself—your truths, your beliefs, your values—benefit others? You are a leader in the lives of your loved ones, at work, and in other areas of life. Think for a moment how the relationship you have with a close friend or significant other differs when you're authentically you versus the person *they* want you to be.

Can you exude true joy when pretending to be someone you're not? Answer: *Hell naw.*

When people see you stand up for what you believe, it inspires trust. No matter the setting, when we observe a person leaning into a topic they have passion around, we tend to sit up and listen a bit more. Even if you don't share the same perspective, don't you feel a greater sense of respect for a person who clearly articulates what they stand for? What we get from this is a pretty good indication this is an individual we can expect will be upfront with us, which is what we deserve.

HELP YOUR RELATIONSHIPS

One of the members of my Fiercely Joyful True Crew is Thomas Dalzell, a senior leader in the federal government and a friend of mine since 2018. Tom is one of those rare people I connected with immediately. We share some of the same beliefs and values, most significantly around the humanity of one another. We both believe everyone should be treated fairly, no matter what they look like or where they come from.

Tom shares two reasons I'd never thought of about why being authentic is important. For those who know us well at work and personally, showing up authentically creates a sense of predictability. Now, I don't necessarily relish in the general thought of being predictable. (I'm all about surprising folk now and then with a totally unexpected reaction or good deed! Keeps things interesting!) In this context, though, I embrace it. Being predictable with our behaviors and thoughts helps our friends and loved ones anticipate our responses.

Remember the birthday when your significant other bought you a gift, sparking absolutely *no* joy, and you know they bought it because you've always *acted like* you love the clothes they buy you, but in fact, they totally don't get your style. Such a bummer! You have yourself to thank because you don't want to hurt their feelings when they gift you an item you know you'll never wear as soon as you see it. You smile and say thank you. If you had let them down gently the very first time it happened, you wouldn't be disappointed on your birthday. The best response the first time is, "Thank you. It's thoughtful of you to take the time to pick out a jacket for me. It's nice but not quite my style. Would you mind if we go to the store together to exchange it for one I love?"

"If I'm not showing up authentically, how can I truly be an ally?"
—THOMAS DALZELL

We've all met them: folks who say one thing and do another. Their words don't match their actions. Nothing erodes trust faster. Tom says people who trust him are looking for him to show up in alignment with his stated beliefs and values. "How can I be out there espousing I believe in equality if I'm not an active participant in supporting it? Regardless of what I look like, regardless of what groups I am associated with, regardless of those types of things, I have to participate."

Don't allow yourself to be silent when it comes to dealing with hard things, y'all. It's those times when it's most important for us to show up.

SECOND CHANCES

Dad is compassionate and believes in second chances. As a business owner, he never has a shortage of people asking for a job. Still, Dad reserves a few positions for men and women getting on solid footing after time behind bars. He's committed to helping people live a life of dignity when society casts them aside. He works directly with what we call the halfway house (where people first transition to after imprisonment but before full release), and they recommend to him the best candidates for his openings. The work is manual and requires heavy lifting, so folks have to be willing to put in hard work.

Let's be real, though. This is both admirable and risky. Dad is willing to take the risk because he believes more people will do the right thing than not. He's right. Every now and then, he catches one stealing and swiftly relieves them of duty. Those occurrences are rare. Instead, most people become part of the Craig & Craig Enterprises team dedicated to getting the work done.

At the very foundation of what we all need is a way to provide for ourselves. Dad wants to take away the stress of finding a good job, giving folks the ability to focus on other areas of their lives needing attention—just like the rest of us are blessed to do.

ALTERNATIVES

Reggie Hubbard and I meet when part of a group writing community. The group embarks on the book-writing journey together and often shares tidbits about what we're writing. When Reggie told me his philosophy about authenticity, I knew I had to talk to him for this book.

"People won't know there's an alternative if we don't give voice to it."

—REGGIE HUBBARD, FOUNDER AND CHIEF
SERVING OFFICER OF ACTIVE PEACE LLC

When Hubbard says this to me, I want to raise my arms and snap my fingers, reminiscent of the days when spoken word events rule my schedule. His words resonate. Consider Hubbard's quote in the context of people who desire to be or do something other than what they see around them. We have different personalities. Someone like me at this stage in life and career will quickly calculate in her mind the risk of doing or saying what I want to do. Then, if I think it's worth it, I do it. On the other hand, some will heed caution and decide if no one else is doing it or saying it, they can't either. We end up missing out on an idea left unspoken. It might have been the one we're seeking. Additionally, a person sits in the space of conformity because we're not encouraging anything else.

"My spoken words, my tone of voice, my written words... are meant to give you space and freedom. That only happens through vulnerability and authenticity." Hubbard is intentional from the start about being in service to others.

How you would *thrive* in such an environment, a place where it's not just okay to be you, it's *invited*?

Open your notebook up again and jot down how you're affected when you believe you have no choice but to make yourself smaller. How would things be different if someone made space for you to be free? When we don't live into who we really are, we lose our sense of self. I don't think we even recognize it until the shift is significant. You get to a point where you no longer remember what *you* want because you're catering to everyone else's idea of who you should be. How can a person show up authentically for anyone else if they can't do it for themselves?

People are watching you. They're watching what you do as a friend, a colleague, a leader, maybe even a manager, a parent, a grandparent, a sister, a brother, a spouse. Others observe and learn from us all the time whether we like it or not—can't control it. What do you want them to see? Someone going along to get along or someone embracing opportunities to engage others as they are? The answer is B.

"I take it very seriously, that the voice I've been given is to be used for the liberation of all beings." Wow. I had to sit back in my chair for a moment. "... the liberation of all beings." Deep. Hubbard embraces a responsibility to help others be *free*. Imma let y'all marinate there for a moment.

There is a collective around you in every segment of your life. In this sense, a collective is a community. You feel more closely aligned with some than others. I offer to you, regardless of the closeness, our responsibility to make space for others to be seen and heard extends to those we disagree with. If we only focus on people who look like us or think like us, we're perpetuating the same problems associated with conformity. Remember Hubbard's quote on giving voice to alternatives. *Everyone* gets to be free, not just your peeps.

WHO'S FIRST?

In a training class, I was introduced to a video about how a movement begins. Posted by Derek Sivers, it's titled, "First Follower: Leadership Lessons from Dancing Guy" (Sivers 2010). In the video, it's a beautiful sunny day, and lots of people are outdoors in a park. Music is playing, and people are socializing, chilling out solo, and the like. Suddenly, one person gets up and starts dancing. Like, for real dancing... picture you or one of your friends dancing at a party when your *favorite* song comes on.

He catches the eye of folks around him. Some stare, probably wondering if he's influenced by something other than the song. Others smile a bit and chat with their buddies about it. It seems like he dances alone in the park for thirty to forty-five seconds. Suddenly, a second person joins him. Dancing guy number two starts dancing like nobody's watching. Soon after the second guy starts, a third person follows, and before you know it, people all over the park are getting their groove on. The takeaway? It isn't the first person or the leader who starts the dance movement. It's the second—the first follower, as Sivers calls him. Once there are two, others are comfortable joining in on the fun. "It was the first follower that transformed a lone nut into a leader. There is no movement without the first follower," says Sivers.

Reflecting for a moment, the slew of dancers bustin' a move after the second person probably had the desire to do so when they saw the first guy. Yet, they didn't. Maybe it felt too risky—they didn't want to be embarrassed, judged, or associated with only the first guy. But once there are two dancers, they feel safe doing a little cabbage patch or whatever dance they choose.

If it's not your style to be the first one to speak up, no problem. Consider being the second—the first follower—they're the ones starting the movement. Taking ownership of supporting others in their authenticity doesn't have to be a grand gesture (but if a grand gesture is your style, by all means, do you!). Start where you're comfortable. You can either tap those toes under the table or shake your shoulders for all to see—it's up to you.

Now, you need to understand going in, if you're the first, you may get no followers. *Zero.* You might be sitting there feeling like you're on a lifeboat all by yourself. Ask yourself, am I willing to take the risk? Think of your values and beliefs. If you don't say anything, does your silence create misalignment for you, or will you remain in integrity with your values? Recognize how much of your thoughts on what you should do are influenced by others versus your gut. Last, it's important to think about potential consequences. Are they insignificant or pretty big? When you're not sure what to do, answer those questions for yourself and then decide.

"The next time you want to withhold your help, or your love, or your support for another for whatever reason, ask yourself a simple question: do the reasons you want to withhold it reflect more on them or you? And which reasons do you want defining you forevermore?"

—DAN PEARCE

KEYS TO BEING FIERCELY JOYFUL:

- ✎ **Take opportunities to engage less vocal folks in conversations.** After you share your thoughts, welcome their input by saying, "So Tom, what do you think?" Or go even further by inviting a contrary opinion: "Tom, do you see this differently?" or, "Tom, if I recall correctly, you had a different perspective on this. Will you share your thoughts?"
- ✎ **Support even when you're not ready to fully commit.** If someone's idea resonates with you, even if you're not sure if it's the right idea, say so. *"Jacinda, I definitely see your point. I think it's valid. I'm on the fence though as to whether it's the best approach."*
- ✎ **Embrace candid discussion.** If you're the one with a contrary opinion and you want to put it out there, go ahead. What matters is it's done with care, respect, and professionalism. "Team, a completely different thought keeps coming to mind for me, so I want to share it. What if we consider…"

🖋 **Stand up for others just as you would yourself.** Don't entertain or empower gossip, talking down to others, or bullying. If someone keeps interrupting others, call them on it. "Jess, let me ask you to hold your thought because Pedro has been trying to weigh in too." If a friend calls you to talk about another friend saying things she wouldn't say to his face, squash it. Same thing goes at work with colleagues. Politely let the gossiper know, "I respect your right to your own opinion. I'm uncomfortable talking about Simone when she's not here to participate in the discussion. You should talk to her directly about your feedback."

You being you results in us all getting to be more of us, which means we get more opportunities to enjoy the uniqueness we each have. Somebody gets to crack dorky jokes. I get to wear my shoulders out. Someone gets to say they're hurting when they are, instead of hiding it because they're afraid to be vulnerable. Someone gets to say their pronouns are they/them/their instead of answering to she/her/hers because their colleagues assume they would. Be you and welcome me.

6

USE YOUR VOICE

It's several years ago, and I'm in an executive meeting at work, though not a principal attendee, sharing an insight sparked by the discussion. I learn later my insight wasn't welcomed because I'm not a peer to those in the room. Before heading into the meeting, where my job is to take notes and record actions, I ask my manager if it's appropriate for me to speak up if I'd like to contribute, and she says, "Absolutely." A few hours later, I learn the executive I directed my insight to was highly offended and wanted to know why I was even speaking at all. Apparently, non-executives shouldn't speak when in meetings with executives. Um... that's stupid. It's hierarchical, egotistical, and leaves on the cutting room floor the value diverse perspectives bring.

Now, I am an executive and don't need permission to speak up. In fact, my colleagues depend on me to do so. Unlike my experience, I invite others to weigh in, no matter their position. Just like we all have things to learn, we also have things to teach.

I didn't expect to talk about George Floyd Jr. in this book. Mr. Floyd is a Black man murdered by a police officer during an arrest in Minneapolis, Minnesota, on May 25, 2020. A store clerk called the police, believing Floyd used a counterfeit $20 bill for his purchase. The police response to the allegation ultimately ended with Floyd's death. Floyd's murder sparked deep outrage across the country and the world. Protests lasted for weeks, even months, in some cities, inspiring an awakening and a movement still alive today against racial injustices. Ironically, Floyd's inability to breathe while he perished under a police officer's knee breathed life into so many others, empowering and imploring us to use our own voices. I pray Mr. Floyd's family and loved ones, especially his daughter, take comfort in knowing his death was not in vain.

HOW GEORGE FLOYD MOVED US

It certainly wasn't the first time a Black man was murdered by law enforcement. Sadly, since 2015, at least 1,394 came before Floyd, and over 300 have come since, according to the *Washington Post*'s "Police Shootings Database" as of December 2022. The database includes only fatal shootings by police. Deaths by other means, such as "police subdual, restraint, and neck compression, which caused his heart and lungs to stop" in the case of Floyd, isn't counted in the database (Forliti, Karnowski, and Webber 2022). And because the Federal Bureau of Investigations does not require reporting police-involved deaths, accurate data is extremely difficult to find. So, what incited an outcry for change this time? It was a perfect storm of events.

First, Floyd's murder occurred just a few months into the COVID-19 pandemic. So many of us were confined to our homes. I was fortunate my work could be accomplished from home. I teleworked with the TV on in the background all day long. It stayed tuned to new channels as I became nearly obsessed with being as informed as possible about COVID-19. Everyone I knew was glued to the TV, trying to figure out how to stay safe and avoid contracting the disease.

So, when Floyd was murdered, we not only heard about it, we also watched it. Most of the day, every day, we watched TV, which gave us a front-row seat to an egregious and horrifying assault lasting nine minutes and twenty-nine seconds. And because we watched with our own eyes, no one was able to skew the narrative to convince us what we saw was justified. It wasn't. People struggled to find a reason for why Floyd was dead other than Derek Chauvin seeing him as unworthy of being treated with human decency because he was a Black man. Truly heartbreaking is the least of what I can call it.

Such an unjust death drove substantive reflection among Americans of all races. For several people I interviewed for this book, Floyd's murder called into question not just the behavior of White people toward people of color but their own behaviors as well. They realized they had been dismissing, ignoring, or simply overlooking inappropriate treatment, which enabled it to continue unchecked. Now, I'm not talking about violence here. I'm talking about the things people say and do related to stereotypes or even personal beliefs, resulting in poor, unfair, or inequitable treatment of those in marginalized populations. Those behaviors leave scars we often never discuss or even acknowledge. So what do we do? How do we fix it? We use our voice.

As I reflect on it, I recall countless instances when I let things go. When a microaggression or flat-out racist statement was made, whether in a group setting or a one-on-one conversation, I'd just let it go. Merriam-Webster.com defines microaggression as: a comment or action that subtly and often unconsciously or unintentionally expresses a prejudiced attitude toward a member of a marginalized group (such as a racial minority). Here are some examples:

- "You are so articulate."
  - When I hear someone say this, it's typically directed to a person of color. I wonder why the person saying it seems surprised. Is it unusual for people of color to be articulate?
- "I don't see color."
  - Um... You must not be looking at me because it's kinda impossible not to see my color. Please understand this, I *want* you to see and *appreciate* my race, not ignore it. It's part of my identity, and I take pride in it. What I don't want is for someone to see my color (or gender) and treat me unfairly, judge me, or dismiss me because of it.

Microaggressions sting whether intentional or not. The time is *now* to stop overlooking or defending them. I believe microaggressions are most often unconscious, meaning my experiences often show people don't have malicious intent. Even so, we need to address it. Now, I say something. I have a conversation to let folks know what I observed and how it made me feel. My feedback is typically well received.

LET ME INTRODUCE MYSELF

It's early in my career, and I don't think I can speak up without facing reprisal. My fear of backlash keeps me silent, unwilling to call out things I know are wrong. Years later, I've built a reputation of integrity, credibility, and reliability, so I have enough cache to speak up. But why did I have to "earn" the right to speak up? Shouldn't we all be able to say what we think and believe in a professional way without fear?

Even when I think I can "get away with it," I don't start speaking my truth for some time because I don't know how. I know I need to be thoughtful about it. Today, you can find all kinds of handbooks and guides for dealing with sexism, racism, and microaggressions. Even just a decade ago, no one was volunteering to teach me, and I didn't ask for help. I took it. I took the hits silently. Smiled at offensive jokes. It chipped away at me little by little. Today, I'm much more mature in my quest to live authentically and refuse to let things go unless I make an intentional decision to do so.

I recently met with officials from another agency and showed up in a way I wouldn't have several years ago. I'm a federal government executive, and the officials from the other agency requested the meeting with me. Two other executives from my agency joined me, and both are one level below me on the org chart in terms of positional seniority. The gentlemen from the other agency are similarly situated, with one being my equivalent. None of us have ever met in person.

One of my colleagues and I walk in together. The three White men from the other agency call out to one of my colleagues, guessing he was the man they'd coordinated with, and introduce themselves and shake hands. They glance at me, don't say a word, and proceed into the conference room. I enter the conference room behind them, introduce myself, and shake their hands, then we sit, beginning the meeting with members of each agency seated on opposite sides of the table.

As the briefing gets underway, I realize the executives from the other agency are making eye contact with only one of my colleagues, also a White male. Even when I speak, they don't look at me. It's as if I'm not even in the room. I believe we teach people how to treat us by the behavior we accept or enable from others. The lack of eye contact and acknowledgment from the other agency executives is disrespectful, so I decide to address it.

I politely interrupt the briefer and ask to pause for a moment. I acknowledge I didn't proactively provide an overview of our roles and responsibilities and would like to ensure clarity on how we'll need to work together to accomplish the mission. Speaking on behalf of my two colleagues, I explain their roles and then inform the visitors I am the executive responsible for ensuring support and approving their requests. I make clear it's important they engage with me as well as my agency colleagues. When I finish, I ask them to continue with the briefing.

Well, what do ya know… suddenly, I'm important enough to be engaged in the discussion. For the rest of the meeting, I receive plenty of eye contact, a few questions, and an ask for support. Following the meeting, the executives send a thank you email addressed to me and copying my colleagues.

I shouldn't have had to call them out, but I did it to stay true to myself. I was not going to make myself small, dim my light, or allow others to minimize the value of my presence. I was intentional and decided in the moment I wouldn't overlook the behavior and be silently frustrated about it. *I used my voice.*

I recognize my colleague could have seized the opportunity to say something. When I discuss it with him afterward, he shares he hadn't noticed what happened. I'm not surprised—he wasn't looking for it. He replays the meeting as we talk and starts to connect the dots. His response? "I'm sorry I didn't catch it, Tash. Our next meeting with them will be virtual. I'll make sure we're in the executive conference room, and you'll be seated at the head of the table so it's crystal clear who's in charge." Yaaasss—see what allies do?

BEING MORE OF WHO YOU ARE MEANT TO BE

"This is literally who you are. You were born this way. This is the way you're supposed to walk around earth. There just is no logical rationale that anyone can give me for why you need to be different."

—KATHY GUZMAN GALLOWAY, FOUNDER AND
CEO OF GALLOWAY CONSULTING, LLC.

Kathy Guzman Galloway spent over fifteen years honing her expertise in branding and marketing strategy while working for some premier large corporations and a few small ones. She'd reached the point when she identified a clear misalignment between the work she was doing and her own values. Galloway decided to make a change. Eventually, she left those lucrative positions to start her own business on her own terms. Additionally, George Floyd's murder prompted Galloway to more fully use her voice to speak up and articulate what is wrong, including when the impact isn't on her but someone else.

The reaction to Floyd's murder is a revelation for Galloway in one amazing way—it brings to light the existing groundswell of support from like-minded people. She feels empowered by it, reminding herself, "It's okay, you can do this. The world is behind me. The world is behind us, in a way we didn't know before simply because we never really talk about it." Her lightbulb moment emboldens Galloway to show up and speak up exactly as she wants to. She will no longer overlook things that need to be called out.

Honestly, doing that, calling a thing a thing is one of my *favorite* things about being authentic. It's my chance to stand firmly upon what I believe in a way that helps others. I get to not just take up space but to *create* it. I get to help others be seen and heard, and that sure feels good.

"Do you lean into your courage to live authentically?" Galloway rejects my premise. "I'm over courage. I'm not trying to find courage because I'll be here all day waiting on it." She shares that the momentum of the world around us helps her. Even though divisiveness has grown across our country, Galloway takes advantage of the doors of support that opened as a result. "All the support and positivity makes me feel like, you know what? I feel like I'm okay; there's actually more people here to support me than are against me." She's willing to accept fear cropping up at times and do what scares her anyway.

In my research, I find similar thinking related to courage and self-confidence. I noticed a movement afoot related to women and confidence. One typical message in the books, articles, videos, etc., is: women simply need to be more confident to get what they want. Shani Orgad and Rosalind Gill, authors of *The Confidence Code: The Science and Art of Self-Assurance—What Women Should Know,* discuss how the tendency to tell women to be more confident lets everyone and everything off the hook for their/its part in creating the obstacles driving the perceived need for women to have greater self-confidence in the first place. There's nothing wrong with self-confidence or courage—in fact, I think both are important and needed. What's wrong is letting everybody off the hook. We *not* go'n do *that*.

I continue to probe, asking if it's Galloway's belief she deserves to be authentic, pushing her to actually do it. "I wouldn't use the word *deserve* because it implies some kind of earning, like I have done something and therefore you owe this to me. In fact, I don't need to do anything. *It's my right.* I owe it to myself to be myself in whatever room I walk into. I walk into a room these days understanding it's my right, whether I know the people in the room or not. This is it. This is what you get. And if this doesn't work for you, that's okay."

Wow. She struck a chord—it's my right! It's *your* right! No permission necessary. Don't ask, just do. Charge accepted.

In a TEDxDMUwomen Talk titled "The Power of Being a Bit More You. How to Find and Use Your Authentic Voice and Why It Matters." Sarah Thomson, director of engagement at De Montfort University, talks about her experience learning to embrace and use her authentic voice and shares her research (Thomson 2020). Thomson describes the start of her journey in which she reached out to a coach for help in modifying how she was engaging and interacting professionally with a goal of being taken more seriously. It took two years, but Thomson's coach helped her see things differently.

"My voice is my tool, and instead of trying to hide or change it, I should use it." —Sarah Thomson, director of engagement at De Montfort University (Thomson 2020).

Thomson's revelation is a powerful one. Quite frankly, in my experience, it's not unusual for members of marginalized groups (women in this case) to focus inward, looking to change something about themselves to resolve a systemic issue. Think about it y'all... let's be real. Women are told and taught "how to be" from childhood to adulthood. We need to stay in our lane, not be too emotional (what in the world does "too emotional" mean anyway? I think it means we shouldn't make others uncomfortable, an idea I wholly reject), not be bossy or aggressive. We're supposed to maintain our composure at all times too. How do these unwritten rules encourage authenticity? They don't.

But waitaminute. Men are told and taught "how to be" from childhood to adulthood too. Be strong. Don't show emotion. You have to be the breadwinner. Be the problem solver—fix everything.

I love the main title of Thomson's piece: "The power of being a bit more you." Woo hoo! Gives me the chills just reveling in agreement: you'll find crazy power in being more of the person you are meant to be. You show up in the uniqueness of you, by being more of you. Adam Grant, Organizational Psychologist at Wharton and #1

NYT bestselling author of *Think Again*, posted on Twitter exactly what you need to know and understand.

"Authenticity is not about being unfiltered. It's about staying true to your principles. The goal isn't to voice every opinion you hold. It's to stand up for ideas that are consistent with your ideals. Being genuine is closing the gap between what you value and what you express" (Grant 2022).

Isn't that fabulous? Grant puts it into perspective perfectly.

KEYS TO BEING FIERCELY JOYFUL:
"The most courageous act is still to think for yourself. Aloud."
—COCO CHANEL

- **"When you're invited to the table, speak."** Rear Admiral (retired) Annie Andrews, one of the first Black women to be promoted to rear admiral, shared her wisdom several years ago when I asked what was one of her most important leadership insights. If you're in a discussion where ideas are being presented or input is asked for, you belong there. Sitting silently gets you and the rest of us nothing, nada, zilch. Speak up and let your voice be heard.
- **Don't agree unless you actually do.** Maybe you verbally disagree or choose silence; listen to your gut and decide what's right for you.
- **Don't laugh or dismiss when someone slights you or others.** Instead, address it productively when the

time is right: "Jeff, I doubt you meant for your statement to be hurtful, but I want you to know it made me feel slighted."

🔑 **Take credit for your work and ideas.** If someone takes your input and rephrases it as their own, say, "Thanks for reframing my idea, Sophie. I'm happy it resonates with you."

🔑 **Expect your input won't be welcome at times and or may be disregarded.** Know it will happen, so you'll be prepared when it does. Don't take it personally, and don't let the behavior deter you from speaking up in the future. Remember, *it's your right!*

7

BE A GIVER

"Life's persistent and most urgent question is, 'What are you doing for others?"

—DR. MARTIN LUTHER KING, JR.

GIVING LESSONS FROM DAD AND MOM

Valentine's Day is an important holiday in my childhood home. Mom loves it, and she wants it to be special. Although she's expressive about her feelings—we know how much she loves us by her words and deeds—Mom goes out of her way searching for the perfect gifts showing her love for us kids. She clears off the desk in the family room and fills it with beautifully wrapped presents for Ellis and me. I love running downstairs on Valentine's Day morning to see it! After a special breakfast, usually pancakes, we head to school and give Valentine's Day cards and candy to our classmates and teachers.

It's a typical first-grade school day, and suddenly, I'm called down to the principal's office. I'm *so* scared. I ask myself, *What did I do?* I replay in my mind the entire morning since stepping on the school grounds, but I can't figure it out. I slow my pace, trying to get to an answer before I arrive, but no luck. I'm so distraught I want to cry. I pause, pull my head up, and prepare to defend myself as I walk through the administration office door.

I'm greeted with a smile from the administrative assistant, who says, "Hello, Natasha, you have a delivery!" while pointing to a huge bouquet of half a dozen red roses. Huh? I'm confused... then relieved... then curious. Roses? For me? Seeing the look on my face, the administrative assistant suggests I read the card. It reads, "Happy Valentine's Day, Darling! I love you today and always. Dad"

I'm grinning from ear to ear, so wide the ladies can see my baby teeth in the back of my mouth. I feel so special and loved. I can't believe Dad did this! I pick up the heavy bouquet, say thank you, and begin my walk back to class.

When I get back, my classmates, mainly the girls, are in complete awe. Their mouths hang open as I carry the flowers to my desk. "Would you like to place your roses on my desk since there's more room?" *Um... not really, because they smell good, and I love all the attention I'm getting!* Alas, the vase takes up way too much space on my tiny desk, and I'm a little afraid of accidentally knocking it over.

I relent and place the bouquet in the middle of my teacher's desk. Then it hits me. I smile, thinking, *Everyone gets to see how beautiful they are now... It's definitely best to share.* From then on, I look forward to my rose delivery on Valentine's Day, which comes without fail until I graduate high school.

Dad had a way of doing things big and small, making people feel special, seen, worthy, or loved. He got as much out of giving to others as the receiver did, which I suspect motivated him to do more.

When I get a little older, I go with Mom to Victoria's Secret countless times. As I pick up lots of items I like, she says, "You're too young to wear anything from here, so put it down." I continue wearing the Hanes six-pack of pastel-colored panties we buy from Kmart. Boring... and far from a fashion statement. And no, I'm planning to show them to anyone (not back then, ha!), but I deserve to feel good about what I'm wearing, even my underwear. After all, it's the foundation of my look! In my early teens, I finally received a few pair of pretty underwear from Victoria's Secret on Valentine's Day. What? I'm crazy excited!

Now, please don't be mistaken, although Mom and Dad love Valentine's Day, they show us love in countless ways year-round. Tight hugs, big smiles welcoming us home, or maybe a surprise batch of cupcakes. No matter the day, we are loved.

It's the week of Valentine's Day when Mom dies on February 11, 1995. I can't bring myself to celebrate the day for a long time afterward because it's not the same without her. Over time, I recognize she would want me to keep celebrating my loved ones. I create new traditions and learn to find joy again in the holiday.

Don't be afraid to give love openly. If it's been a minute since you've shown or expressed love to those you hold dear, today is the perfect time to do it.

———

"I've learned that people will forget what you said, people will forget what you did, but people will never forget how you made them feel."

—DR. MAYA ANGELOU

GIVE INTANGIBLES

I used to joke with a close friend, John Campbell, "What I love most about you is the intangibles you bring to our friendship!" Some of the best gifts I've received are those without a price tag and often no physical form. John is hilarious and easily puts a smile on my face. Who doesn't love the gift of laughter? He's one of the most intelligent people I know, making spending time talking with him enriching. He's also got an uncanny ability to imagine himself in someone else's shoes. Because he does, John is compassionate and gives folks grace. What comes to mind first when I think of him are these amazing characteristics (read on to Chapter 11 to learn more on why John is part of my chosen family).

When I walk down the street minding my own business and people watching, it lifts my spirit when someone takes the time to say they like my outfit, my hair looks beautiful, or they simply smile and say hello. I'm known for spotting a fashionista and not letting him or her get away without a compliment. Seeing them smile makes me happy. Those moments are sweet gifts, and I enjoy giving and receiving. My personal rule is if I make eye contact with someone I'm passing by, I greet them and smile. Who knows if they're having a great day or a horrible one? Or, maybe I'm the only person to offer them a smile. A tiny bit of effort can make someone's day.

A friend from my True Crew (Chapter 11) says when we come across someone our gut tells us is special, we should act on it. "If you feel in your spirit they have potential, pour into them. Don't be afraid to give them a little advice because chances are they need to hear from you."

GIVE FORGIVENESS

One of the greatest gifts we can give to ourselves and others is forgiveness. In Chapter 1: Becoming Me, I share my experience forgiving my dad. I learn forgiveness is a gift we give to ourselves, not others. Forgiving someone isn't excusing what they've done—it's not a pass. I used to think of it as a pass, which is why I struggled to forgive earlier in life. I understand now forgiveness is showing compassion for me and perhaps the wrongdoer. For some of us, the latter seems a bridge too far. If you're thinking, *They don't deserve compassion from me,* consider this insight from *Psychology Today*'s article "5 Reasons Why It's Important to Forgive":

"Forgiveness helps your health. Negative emotions rob your energy and take a toll on your body, mind, and spirit. Anger, anxiety, depression, and undue stress generate a negative influence on your body. These can cause elevated blood pressure, heart rate, and the feeling of being out of control. The intensity can run the gamut, from mild discomfort to very intense physical reactions" (Brenner 2020).

Compelling, right? Forgiveness is a choice, which means we hold the power to do what serves us well. Remember, forgiveness does not require maintaining a relationship or reconciling with the person who wronged you. However, it becomes challenging to sever a relationship you can't escape, such as those with family members or the mother of your child. What works for me is remembering to show up in alignment with my values. I won't tolerate allowing others to influence me negatively. Respect is part of my value system, which means I'll be cordial. What I won't do is spend more time than necessary engaging with someone I don't want to talk to. Again, do what serves you well.

GIVE KINDNESS: THE CHRISTMAS CONCERT

"Be the reason someone smiles. Be the reason someone feels loved and believes in the goodness in people."

—ROY T. BENNETT, AUTHOR OF *THE LIGHT IN THE HEART*

Applying to Howard University is a last-minute decision coming after my visit to the campus for homecoming in 1991. My twin cousins, Cynthia and Karen, are students, and the family encourages me to visit. As one might imagine, homecoming on most college campuses is an amazing time—not just the parties but the energy and excitement. I fall in love with Howard in one weekend. On Sunday, we go to the chapel for service. The Howard University Community Choir is singing. I'm lifted up by their voices in the most exhilarating way. In addition to deciding I'm going to Howard, I'm going to be part of that choir too.

I love singing! It brings me joy. I sing in the Bethel AME Church in Scranton, Pennsylvania, during my teenage years. The thing is, I'm not good—at least not when singing alone. On the other hand, I can stay in tune when singing along with others. Completely aware of my limitations, I refuse to let them stop me. No one in their right mind would ever call me a natural-born singer! But... among a choir? I can blow!

When freshman year begins, I stalk notice boards on campus waiting for my shot. Eventually, I see it: Open Call for Auditions for the Howard University Community Choir

(HUCC). I arrive early, stunned by how many people are trying out. My stomach sinks. *Girl,* do not *let your nerves get the best of you. Nothing beats a fail but a try.* They call my name and I give it my all, which turns out to be a loud and off-key audition.

The choir director tilts his head and squints, furrowing his brows. My guess? He's wondering if I have any clue how terrible I sing. *Have mercy, was I that bad? Say something, please!* "I can't believe I'm saying this, but I'll allow you join rehearsals. You need *werk*—lots of it. I expect you to practice every day on your own too. Understand, you are *not* a choir member, but if you show significant improvement, I may revisit my decision." Thomas Pierre, our amazing director, later told me my energy and passion convinced him to give me a chance—and, he confessed, "You were the worst audition of the day!"

I don't miss a single rehearsal, and I practice daily in my dorm stairwell because the acoustics are *awesome* (bet my neighbors don't enjoy it as much as I do, tee hee!). My hard work pays off! I become an official member of the Howard University Community Choir a couple months after auditioning. We sing on campus, all across the DC area, and up and down the East Coast. I make fast friends with other members. It's an experience I treasure and won't forget.

We're preparing for our annual Christmas concert on campus. Mom is too sick to travel. Thomas is excited Dad is coming and knows how much it means to me. He surprises me, "I'm giving you a brief solo part in one of the songs—you better nail it." *Eek! Wow!*

I'm a ball of nerves when the day arrives. *Please Lord, help me get through this.* Dad is enjoying himself, getting up occasionally to clap or sway. When I step up to the mic, Dad rises. The song is slow, which means no dancing. Instead, he stands tall and still with his hands clasped and a few tears rolling down his cheek. He's proud, and I am too.

We make our way downstairs after the performance for prayer. Dad hands a single red rose to each choir member as we enter the room. What an awesome surprise! The guys are a little uncomfortable yet excited, most receiving a rose for the first time. He expresses his gratitude for the concert and congratulates us. When we get outside, there's a limousine waiting! Me and my friends jump into our fancy ride feeling like queens and kings. Dad treats us to dinner. We have an amazing time—it's the perfect ending to a perfect day.

I felt special and loved after the concert night experience. I know many of my fellow choir members won't forget it. Everyone deserves those kinds of experiences. Dad's kindness toward me and others throughout his life proved how single, caring moments can make a huge impact on someone's life. What a gift! And it's one we can all afford to give because kindness doesn't have to cost a dime. Now, how about smiling and saying hello to the people you walk by tomorrow? You'll make someone's day!

GIVE RESPECT

It's the early 1990s and I'm starting my new cashier job at Roy Rogers. Roy Rogers is a fast-food chain and known for its roast beef sandwiches. I'm working at the location in the Dupont Circle area of NW Washington, DC. Most of our customers are from the big corporate offices filling the area.

Lunch rush is overwhelming. Lines stretch to the door, and people want to get in and out quickly. It's in my nature to greet people with full eye contact, hello, and a smile. I'm amazed at how many customers don't return the favor. No hello and no eye contact at all. I chalk it up to people being in a hurry or maybe having a bad day.

It's still my first week, and I'm working as quickly as I can. I take the next order, extend my hand to accept the customer's cash, and he sets it down on the counter right next to my hand. I think to myself, *Okay, that's weird. Maybe he didn't see my hand. Oh well.* And then it happens again and again and again. I'm floored because I recognize the behavior is done with intention. It's disrespectful. Why won't they simply place their money in my hand which I *know* they see is extended?

Soon I realize I'm not seen by many of the customers, meaning, not seen as worthy of basic respect. People often are rude. I'm experiencing them behaving as if they're better than me. *Who do they think they are?* It zaps my energy to put on a happy face for those unwilling to acknowledge me. The disrespect typically comes from people working in white collar jobs as evidenced by their suits or other office attire. On the other hand, I wear a uniform. Patrons who wear uniforms tend to be kind and respectful with few exceptions.

Experiences from those days at Roy Rogers taught me the importance of giving respect to others, no matter the setting, person's job, background, etc., *Everyone* deserves respect. At work, I know the names of the janitorial staff and we chat most days. They're on my holiday gift list. I see people walk past them like they're invisible and then say hello to someone else they pass by who isn't in a uniform. At times, we fail to realize there is always a circle in which we won't be welcomed. Maybe some think they've "arrived" because they have a white-collar career with a great compensation package. Step into a room of C-suite executives or millionaires and see if you're treated as an equal. Been there and felt the sting of the questions essentially boiled down to *How'd you get in here?*

Giving respect is one of the easiest things we can do, and it doesn't cost a thing.

GIVE YOUR FAVORITE THINGS

I celebrate Christmas. It brings me tons of joy to do a little something for my friends and colleagues during the holiday season. I used to make gifts (such as a hand-knit scarf or body scrub), but it started to feel too stressful. Being a procrastinator, I was overwhelmed trying to get hand-made gifts ready in time, so I made a change for my own well-being. Now, I give gifts meeting two criteria: first, it's something I love (meaning I'd buy it for myself), and second, it's from a small business (absolutely love being intentional about supporting the small business owners in my own community as much as possible). Remember, gift giving is about the sentiment, not the price tag.

One of my recent obsessions is a local business here in Washington, DC, called hunnybunny boutique. The owners are two young girls, Nya and Zuri, who create by hand all-natural bath and beauty products. They run the business with help from their mom. I love the products I've tried and give them to colleagues and loved ones as a little holiday cheer. The fact these gifts come with a story makes them a perfect choice. Fingers crossed, a byproduct might be some new business for Nya and Zuri!

My husband, Edwaun, was born and raised on the South Side of Chicago. If you haven't met anyone from Chicago, you might not know they love their hometown as much as Texans love their state. Chicago is full of rich history and culture—and my husband doesn't let more than a day or two go by without reminding me. Lol. If you've been to the city, you might know it's not only famous for its deep-dish pizza. Chicago is the home of Garrett's Popcorn. My husband's favorite is the Chicago Mix, which has perfect proportions of caramel and cheese popcorn. He loves it so much, he orders a couple dozen or so canisters during the holidays to give to friends and colleagues. He enjoys giving it as much as people enjoy eating it.

Giving gifts is one of my favorite things, especially when I give something uniquely suited for the receiver. My friend loves dragonflies, so I gift her a beautiful pair of dragonfly earrings and a matching necklace for her birthday. She loves them so much, they go from the box to her earlobes immediately. My heart smiles a few minutes later when someone compliments her jewelry. We both grin wide enough for our baby teeth to show.

I've learned in recent years my way of giving is sometimes different from what people expect. Our parents drilled into us kids we should always give without looking for anything in return. I still approach giving this way. I get excited and giddy when I give gifts. If it's tangible, I can't wait to see the recipient's reaction! When I give authentically, with no expectation of reciprocation, it brings me joy.

Even though I don't want anything in return, people often feel an obligation to do something in return. We all expect acknowledgment of the gifts we give—a simple thank you will do. If we send a thank you card, we totally make the gift giver's day! On the other hand, some people look for tangible reciprocation demonstrating gratitude. Be aware of how you feel about this and choose to give accordingly. If you think a person you're considering giving to will not appreciate your kindness, you may decide not to do it. It's completely up to you. What's most important here is giving because you want to give. If you don't really feel the desire to give, but instead you feel obligated, listen when your spirit tells you the giving isn't in alignment with your values.

GIVING HELPS YOU JUST AS MUCH AS OTHERS

Did you know there are health benefits associated with giving? Yes, y'all, it's been scientifically proven through research. Cleveland Clinic's *healthessentials* discusses the benefits shared by Dr. Susan Albers in "Why Giving is Good for Your Health" (2022). "When we do things for other people, it makes us feel much more engaged and joyful," says Albers. As described in the article, a chemical response occurs in your body when you do nice things, and your brain secretes "feel good" chemicals (Health Essentials Staff 2022).

This rings true for me. I'm blessed to know how it feels to receive thoughtful gifts. I want to share the same feeling with others. I'm a kid in a candy store, all giddy and excited when I have an inkling to do something I know will make someone smile and/or feel valued.

Dr. Albers shares four benefits—both mental and physical—people experience as a result of giving: lower blood pressure, a longer lifespan, less stress, and a "helper's high," which boosts self-esteem, increases happiness, and knocks down feelings of depression (Health Essentials Staff 2022). Aren't those attractive benefits? Of course they are! To think we can gain benefits by simply giving, and then add on the feel-good chemical response—definitely worth it.

If you're inspired by emotional or spiritual benefits, here's another perspective on what giving does for you. In "4 Big Reasons to Put Service At the Center of Your Life," Nate Sanna sums it up beautifully. He suggests looking at serving others, or giving of yourself, as a way of life instead of an activity. For me, living in service to others is part of who I am, so I completely agree. Sanna believes life can be more fulfilling when you approach "everything you do in a spirit of service," and here's how he describes the transformation:

- "You become wealthy when you serve others—your financial success is linked to what you give
- You learn and grow more when you serve—you gain new perspectives
- You become happier—you shift your focus to others, feel needed, and help solve problems that broaden your experiences
- You change the world—meaningful change starts with just one person, family, or community" (Sanna 2020).

Whew! The last bullet, "You change the world," has me shaking my shoulders again. How amazing would it be to have a small part in making our world a better place? Even if we think a bit more pragmatically, influencing meaningful change for just one person is priceless.

Being a giver brings me such joy! I attribute it to the positivity associated with giving, whether gifts are intangible or take up space, giving feeds the soul. Now that you know what to give and how good giving is for you, go on and get busy!

"You give but little when you give of your possessions. It is when you give of yourself that you truly give."

—KAHLIL GIBRAN

- 🔑 **Give kindness**—At work, we have a small convenience store open a few hours a day. They have a popcorn machine. Some days, I just hear the buttery popcorn calling my name, so I'll head upstairs in between meetings to get some. When I'm leaving the office area, more often than not, I ask whoever is there if they want anything from the store. I'm already going, so why not save someone else a trip? It's such a small gesture, yet I enjoy extending it, and my colleagues appreciate the offer.

- 🔑 **Give support**—There are times when we want someone to just listen, not fix or solve, listen. Another way to support people is to check on them from time to time. Send a text or give them a call and just ask, "How are you?" That shows you care.

- 🔑 **Give time**—Offer to cut your neighbor's grass. Good with numbers? Volunteer to help a charity with accounting work. If you're in event planning, give your friend some ideas for hosting her son's high school graduation party. Think of your superpowers—the things you do very well with ease—and look for opportunities to share your talents with others.

- 🔑 **Give compassion and grace**—Giving grace is giving empathy and compassion. Beating yourself up after a mistake doesn't change what happened. Focus on the learning instead. Do the same for others. When we consider one's intentions rather than only their actions, we're giving grace. When someone makes a huge mistake after we told them it would happen, we're giving grace (and putting aside our pettiness!) when we forgo saying, "I told you so." Take time to put yourself in someone else's shoes, or maybe your own, and give grace.

8

BE GRATEFUL

"The secret to having it all is believing you already do."

—JOHN ASSARAF

For the last decade of my life, I've thrived in a space of gratitude. I sometimes close my eyes and stop for a few moments to acknowledge the blessings bestowed upon me. During those reflections, my body fills with warmth, and a sense of calm comes over me. And I'm tellin' y'all, the more grateful I am, the more blessings come my way! I realize now I've been this way as long as I can remember: what my parents worked to instill is us took hold at a very young age.

My parents raised me to have an abundance mindset. Abundance means "an ample quantity" according to the Merriam-Webster.com. I'm a glass-half-full kinda girl. Believing in abundance helps me continuously feel gratitude. For example, I believe there is room for *everyone* to succeed, which means I'm happy to celebrate others' accomplishments without thinking they create a lack of opportunity for me. I know I have everything I need and more.

One key attribute of an abundance mindset is generosity. In Chapter 7, I discuss how giving to others makes me feel amazing. I get a feeling of fullness when I serve. My brother and I learn early on that we have a responsibility to serve others. In our parents' eyes, life isn't about prosperity for oneself but prosperity for all. Volunteering is required in our household from a young age. I remember in high school leading an effort to write letters to soldiers in Kuwait during Operation Desert Storm. My brother is a Marine serving in the war. He writes to us often, and I cherish receiving his letters and responding to them. I want other soldiers to get a letter too. My fellow students show up in a big way, and we mail hundreds of letters to men and women protecting and serving us.

My mom volunteers at the Women's Resource Center in Scranton, Pennsylvania. It's an organization helping people safely remove themselves from abusive situations. It isn't unusual for the phone to ring in the middle of the night with a call for my mom's support. She gets up every time to be by the side of a woman whose name she doesn't know but who desperately needs her support. The Women's Resource Center later name an annual award after Mom because of her dedication and commitment to service.

When my grandmother, Nana, is stricken with lung cancer and a brain tumor, she moves in with us so Mom can care for her. Mom is at work during the day, and Nana can't make it downstairs to the kitchen. Before I go to school, a driver from Meals on Wheels brings a meal for Nana. I put the foil tin on top of the radiator in Nana's room to keep it warm until she's ready to eat. I'm not sure what we would do if we didn't have those meals every weekday.

I'm so grateful, I later become a Meals on Wheels volunteer driver, delivering meals once per week. I love seeing the brightened faces of those looking out their window watching me walking toward their home. I'm just as excited to see them and spend a few minutes chatting. It's not unusual for me to be the only visitor some of them see until their next delivery, which saddens me. Still, I'm happy I can put a smile on their faces while I'm on duty.

Just five years later, when Mom's cancer comes out of remission, her doctors want her to undergo another surgery and more treatments. The timing is terrible because Mom's disability income ended, and she's no longer able to afford medical insurance. We're overwhelmed. One day the doorbell rings, and it's Mom's manager from work. I invite him in. "I don't plan to stay long, just wanted to give you this, Sharon." He hands Mom a cashier's check worth enough to keep us afloat for months. "Several colleagues contributed. We know times are difficult. We wish we could do more but hope this will ease some of the pressure." He expresses to Mom they're grateful for her not only as an employee but as a friend who cares for and supports them beyond what work requires.

Oh my goodness! I'm stunned people would be so kind and generous. My mom is more shocked than me and overcome with gratitude of her own. Tears flow while she hugs her manager tightly, asking him to tell everyone how thankful she is and promising to pray for the blessing to return to each of them. *If I become half the woman Mom is, I will be proud.*

When Mom dies in February 1995, it seems life is at a standstill. Still, even then, at twenty years old, it doesn't take long for my mindset to shift. I'm heartbroken my Mom died so young. She was just forty-nine—the age I am when I write *Fiercely Joyful.* As distraught as I am while grieving, I can't help but recognize the twenty years I *did have* with her were amazing. I treasure my memories and the experiences we had together. I have friends who don't know their mother, have an estranged or abusive relationship. What I get to remember is feeling loved unconditionally, laughing together, and shopping with Mom and Nana every Saturday at McCrory's, Kmart, and Woolworths.

The other thing striking me is the appreciation of all the small stuff. My bedroom in my teen years is right next to Mom's, so we share a wall. At night, the simple act of going to bed is an event we're both grateful for! Strange, right? We giggle with excitement getting into bed and enjoying cozying up in our blankets. "It's bedtime! My blanket is so warm!" Back and forth, we exclaim our joy through the wall. Guess what? I still do this—not every night, but at least several times a year. Even after over ten years together, my husband still looks at me with curiosity wondering why I'm so excited about going to sleep! Nowadays, I think it's twofold. I love when my skin hits my soft sheets, and I remember giggling with joy about it with Mom.

One of Dad's favorite meals is veal piccata. We love Mom's veal! When she cooks it (in an electric skillet... I know, I'm dating myself!), she gets excited about making the "gravy" at the end, which she calls *gook* (pronounced like hook). She does a little dance while stirring it up in the pan. Mom adds lots of green onions, which I looooove. I'm right there dancing along with her! She plates the food, and I ask for "Extra gook, please!" Why on Earth does she call it gook? I dunno, y'all, 'cause nothin' about gook sounds appetizing! Nevertheless, it sure puts a smile on my face and some pep in my step when I know we're having veal with gook for dinner.

I grow up in Scranton, Pennsylvania. When my parents separate and divorce, my brother Ellis and I get jobs in the city to help Mom pay the bills. We can no longer afford my dance classes, which I've taken for nine years. Dancing makes me feel free. The thought of giving it up is devastating for both me and Mom. "I hope you'll be able to start class again soon, but for now, you'll have to dance at home." I'm sad not just because I can't go to class anymore but seeing Mom so upset about being unable to pay for it. It's one of many lessons of sacrifice.

My part-time job is at the Jewish nursing home, where my Mom also works part-time. She has janitorial duties, and I work in the kitchen as a dishwasher. On occasion, I'm asked to serve food to the residents in the dining room.

Those are my favorite days because I love interacting with them. I make a few special connections, and I make an effort to visit those residents during my breaks. Spending time with them, talking about their favorite memories or my latest happenings in school, brings me a sense of joy. I'm grateful they're so happy to see me. The noticed when I'm not there, too. After an extra day off, I'd hear, "Where have you been, Natasha? We missed you!"

I'm happy I've learned to be grateful for both little and big things. I don't need grandiose or expensive things to experience joy. What gives you a sense of excitement? Giddiness? For me, the feeling of sunshine on my skin. Underwear that don't ride, ice-cold water mixed with Crystal Light, and my talented eyebrow threader—all things I am grateful for.

WHY GRATITUDE MATTERS

Did you know researchers have scientifically proven the benefits of gratitude? Yaaasss... this isn't what Tash thinks. Folks have studied this, and data confirms it. I attest to the findings because being grateful has literally changed my life.

In "Giving thanks can make you happier," published in Harvard Health Publishing's *HealthBeat* newsletter, we learn, "In positive psychology research, gratitude is strongly and consistently associated with greater happiness. Gratitude helps people feel more positive emotions, relish good experiences, improve their health, deal with adversity, and build strong relationships" (2021).

So how do you get there? You cultivate and grow gratitude. The more you express gratitude, the more you'll have. Gratitude is a positive emotion. If fills me up in a way tough to describe. It's almost akin snuggling into a cozy blanket by the fire on a cold winter day. It's soothing and comforting.

Being grateful brings me joy. When I feel joy, with it comes a sense of peace. In those moments when life is really hard, I can still find joy. When I'm not feeling happy, perhaps when I'm feeling down or even depressed, I still experience joy. Joy is a *choice*, and I choose it every single opportunity I get. No one can take my joy from me unless I'm willing to give it away.

KEYS TO BEING FIERCELY JOYFUL:

- **Make time for gratitude daily.** I'll be the first to say the idea of journaling appeals to me, yet it's been challenging to commit to it! I finally found an approach I can stick with. Spend five minutes daily (morning or evening, you choose what works best) either reflecting on or writing down three things you're grateful for. This has been very easy for me to build into my daily routine of planning my day, which I accomplish the night before.
- **Not feeling particularly grateful? Reframe.** I learned this technique from one of my coaches, Desiree Osorio Strong, a well-being habits specialist I work

with through BetterUp. In the simplest of terms, she taught me to look at situations, thoughts, and feelings from a different perspective. Don't think small about what you can accomplish, think big. Don't think scarcity, think abundance. Fear failure? Reframe it. Our growth and learning comes in the midst of struggles and falling down. The important part isn't how many times you fall but continuing to get up and try again.

"Failure should be our teacher, not our undertaker. Failure is delay, not defeat. It is a temporary detour, not a dead end. Failure is something we can avoid only by saying nothing, doing nothing, and being nothing."

—DENIS WAITLEY

- **Be present.** Being present helps us be fully engaged. Whether it's stopping to watch the sun set or putting your phone aside when talking with your partner, being present means we can more readily acknowledge the joy in each moment rather than focus on a future we can't control or a past we can't change.
- **Embrace opportunities.** The world is full of possibility! I'm guilty of being less than eager to seize them. I've been practicing, though. I'm saying yes more often even when I'd rather binge on Netflix. The result? Abundant blessings! It never fails, y'all. I get something in return and feel gratitude. Make a short list of opportunities you will embrace in the next ninety days and get ready!

9

POLISH YO'SELF

"Dress shabbily and they remember the dress. Dress impeccably and they remember the woman."

—COCO CHANEL

A LESSON FROM MOM

It's probably the early to mid-eighties. Dad *loves* giving gifts, both big and small. Rarely a day passes when he doesn't bestow something upon someone, even if it's a cup of coffee. He loves secretly picking up the tab for the table next to us at a restaurant even if we only exchanged a greeting. Dad loves making people smile. He instills that in me, too.

Dad has a *big* gift in mind for Mom—a mink fur coat. I know, I know; this was over thirty-five years ago. Today, it would *definitely* be faux fur! From many recountings of the story by my parents, I recall there are two prominent fur coat stores in Scranton. Dad tells Mom to go try some furs on and choose what she wants. He'll make the pricey purchase after her mind is made up. Mom is looking around in the first store when an associate says, "We don't have anything here you can afford." The pounding in Mom's chest quickens, and she's so close to *cussing the associate out.* Mom's prolonged glare speaks volumes. Still steaming as she exits, the door sticks, letting in the frigid air that cools tears she can no longer hold back.

Mom vows to never step foot in the store again. She's convinced the unacceptable treatment came from them judging her by the jeans, T-shirt, and Nike sneakers she wore. The next day, Dad goes to the other fur coat store, selects a $2,000 mink he knows Mom will love, and purchases it with cash. He picks Mom up and, despite her protests, heads to the store she visited. With her new full-length mink draped around her shoulders, Dad escorts Mom inside and asks for the store manager. He describes Mom's experience, then says, "Your loss." And they walk out. #MicDrop

The sobering and emotional experience makes it clear to Mom how much we are judged by our appearance. Although she talked about her clothes influencing the store associates, I believe her race and Afro hairstyle were factors, too. Mom's personal philosophy on presenting herself evolves, and she decides to present her best self to increase the probability of being judged favorably from the start. Mom looks "put together" *all* the time now. She dresses appropriately *and* impeccably for every occasion: work, church, high school football games, a Broadway play, or a volunteer event. Her clothes, hair, makeup, nails, and accessories are always pristine. Even Mom's casual look is timeless and classic and doesn't include sweatpants of any kind!

I adopt Mom's philosophy in my own way. Taking pride in my appearance and being happy with my look boosts my confidence. I set my clothes and accessories out every work night. On occasion, after getting dressed, I check the mirror, and what I see ain't sparkin' any joy: *this is so* not *cute.* Walking out the door happy with how I'm presenting starts my great day right. Even if it means I'll be a few minutes late, I click undo, pull an ensemble that works every time, and get ta rocking the day.

As I wrap up Mom's lesson, the Pew Research Center offers related data in its report O*n Gender Differences, No Consensus on Nature vs. Nurture.* They found Americans have different expectations for men and women. Approximately 35 percent of respondents shared traits associated with a woman's physical appearance are what society values most. For men, the top answer from 33 percent of respondents was honesty and morality (Parker, Menasce, and Stepler 2017). I'm not surprised by the data, but disappointed for sure.

Whether you're a man, woman, or nonbinary, appearance discrimination or bias is problematic. In an ideal world, we'd take time to get to know what's on the inside of a person ahead of making judgments. We're not there... yet. Acknowledging what we know to be true and then working together to address challenges can further progress for all.

In her book, *Executive Presence: The Missing Link Between Merit and Success*, Sylvia Ann Hewlett's research reveals three pillars of executive presence: how you act (gravitas), how you speak (communication), and how you look (appearance) (2014, 5). I have about fifty-six tabs lining the pages of the book—it resonates *that* much! I apply the concepts to life—personally and professionally. Yes, I'm an executive at my day job, which is why I first picked up the book. However, our presence matters in every aspect of life. In this chapter, I'll share insights of my own and others aligned with Hewlett's three pillars. We get *one* first impression. It's important to leave a positive and lasting one that's authentically yours, and you have the power to make it so.

HOW YOU BEHAVE (GRAVITAS)

The colleagues I work with from 2009–2012 are big fans of former First Lady Michelle Obama, whom I also hold in high regard. I admire her poise, wisdom, style, grace, sense of humor, and authenticity. (And yes, even 'dem arms! Again, I digress) Simply put, I love her presence. Despite our politics, many agree she's an amazing woman. So when my coworkers nickname me "Michelle" because how I carry myself reminds them of her, naturally I'm flattered, right? Wrong.

I'm annoyed. I don't deserve such a compliment. "Stop calling me Michelle, please!" One coworker says, "Why?

You're *our* Michelle! You make us proud just like she does."
Although my reaction surprises them, they fall in line
like great colleagues do. From my perspective, it's inappropriate to have Mrs. Obama's name attributed to me
because her accomplishments and impact far outweigh
mine. I don't lack self-confidence, yet I have never thought
to compare myself to the former first lady. Like, not *evah*.

It's been nearly ten years since I was nicknamed Michelle.
I've grown since, developing pride in my gifts and contributions to the world around me. Acknowledging what
makes me special, including my welcoming and support-
ive presence, is comfortable now. If someone paid me the
same compliment today, I'd acknowledge it, be humbled,
and thank them. What a blessing my colleagues thought
of me in such a way! Today it makes me smile and warms
my heart.

I *love* the word gravitas (pronounced graa-vuh-taas)! The
pronunciation makes me shake my shoulders a little bit
when I say it out loud. Feels fancy. So what is it? Here's
how Merriam-Webster.com defines gravitas: high seri-
ousness (as in a person's bearing or in the treatment of a
subject). Hmm. Maybe gravitas is a "use it in a sentence"
kind of word because that definition doesn't at all give
me the fancy feeling I just mentioned.

Hewlett largely uses stories from her research rather than
a precise definition to illustrate what gravitas means. She

also shares the top aspects of gravitas according to the senior leaders she interviewed (2014, 16).

- Confidence
- Decisiveness
- Integrity
- Emotional Intelligence
- Reputation
- Vision/Charisma

Starting to come together? Ever been in a room when someone you don't know captures your attention, drawing you right in? Maybe it's their energy, how other people greet them, or the way they command the room. I bet you've heard people say, "There's something about him that I really like," but they can't put their finger on the "something." It's gravitas (shakes shoulders again)!

Do you see where we're going? Presence isn't only what's on the outside. The unseen is just as important. Elsa Powel Strong is vice president of solution strategy at Ariel, which means her job is helping people build influence and communication skills, largely accomplished through personal presence. In her article, "The Power of Personal Presence," she defines it this way:

"Personal presence is the ability to connect authentically with others—both their hearts and their minds—so they feel included, engaged, and empowered. Three key—and complementary—skills of personal presence are authenticity, emotional intelligence and self-awareness" (Strong, 2022).

Let's break this down. Authenticity is about showing up in alignment with your core values. Nearly every time I speak to a large audience, I'm told my authenticity or realness shines through. Hearing that input is humbling and brings me joy. And y'all, lots of those events have been virtual. People saw me on camera from my shoulders up. Now, don't get it twisted. Unattached (bright coral) Fenty lipstick is my signature shade, and my face is always beat for an event, but more is required to make a meaningful impression. It comes down to how I deliver my message and how it makes people feel.

Emotional intelligence is identifying and managing not just your own emotions but those of others, too. Yep... means we have to think about how what we say and do impacts others. Once again, it's not all about us. If I'm being thoughtful, I'm considering you and everyone else who will hear my message. Saying, "This isn't what I wanted. Why didn't you do what I asked?" lands differently than "I wonder if my request was unclear because I was expecting a different outcome." I can't think of anyone in my circle who enjoys being blamed for anything. Our natural response is defensiveness. But, owning the fact that perhaps you didn't provide the specificity necessary to get what you wanted? Defenses down.

Speaking of self-awareness, do you know your triggers? Things people say or do that immediately frustrate you? One of my major pet peeves at work is when someone explains a misstep, and they blame everyone except themselves. Ain't nobody perfect. We need to own our part of failures. Dang... as I write this, I have to acknowledge what I'm complaining about could be of my own doing!

Looking in the mirror for a moment, when this happens, I need to ask myself if I've created a space where folks feel comfortable owning their stuff. Or, are people worried about my reaction and thus unwilling to own their part? My point is, there's blame to go around. Rarely is anyone completely without fault when things go awry. Since this is one of my triggers, I need to be mindful of how I react when it happens. Gotta keep my face in check (I'm not a poker player) and avoid rushing to judgment.

Bottom line? Be mindful of your gravitas or personal presence. There's one of you in this world. Lean into your authenticity, be self-aware, and practice emotional intelligence, showing up as the best version of you.

EVEN IF WE DON'T LIKE IT, APPEARANCE MATTERS

Knowing we're judged by our looks presents an opportunity for us to choose what consideration we give to our physical appearance. I've been overweight most of my life. Some people assume I'm lazy and a poor eater. I had a seizure over a decade ago and was required to take anti-seizure medication unless I wanted to give up driving. The medicine has a well-known side effect of weight gain. During a check-in with my neurologist, she raised concern about an eight-pound increase in my weight. "I want you to start exercising at least three times a week." Raising my eyebrows in surprise at her assumption, I shared, "I ran ten miles yesterday. I'm training for a marathon, running five days a week. I think I'm good on exercise." Seeing her shock, I offer to show her my Garmin watch stats. "Not necessary." *Aw, how nice of her to take my word for it.*

The doctor judged me by my appearance and made assumptions about my health habits. Not cool. However, can any of us say we *never* judge folks upon first look? Not me. I strive to be mindful enough to catch myself doing it and then adjust accordingly. Rather than assume, she could have asked me to share my exercise routine. I wouldn't have clapped back on that!

One of my friends tells me, "Focus on appearance doesn't resonate with me. It's not something I've ever focused on. I focus on the long game, and people learn the value I bring." My response is, "Your approach to your appearance is a luxury people of color don't typically have." My friend is a White man. Now, I'm not saying White men aren't judged by their appearance because we all are. The difference is people of color usually don't get a pass. If my look conveys I don't take much pride in my appearance, I'm more likely to be written off, whereas my friend isn't.

I don't want bias based on appearance to change me or you. Don't want it to hold us back either. What works for me is being conscious of it and modulating accordingly when I expect it will serve me well. Sometimes, we equate modulating our behaviors with a lack of authenticity. Not true! For example, let's say I cuss a lot. Cussing at work ain't okay... so I curb it when I'm on the clock. That's not inauthentic, that's being professional. I love *bling*! On almost everything. Do I show up to work in a sequined suit on any ol' Wednesday? No sir or ma'am, I do not. Although...maybe for the after-hours holiday party! I embrace my bling in a way that's appropriate for my workplace. My glittery pen, gold monogrammed notebook, and my phone case li'l bit of gold glitter on it are office staples. Don't abandon everything that brings you joy, just do it thoughtfully.

<hr />

MY CROWN

For many years, Black women wearing our hair as it grows naturally or in hairstyles embraced by Black culture (such as cornrows) were seen as unprofessional. In my experiences, most things not conforming to the ideals of White America seemed to be thought of as unprofessional. We're in the 2020s, y'all: if your hair is clean and neat, it's professional. Period. Sadly, adopting that mindset took me a long time and was a tough road.

Remember all that running I've been doing? Getting ready for work after morning runs is brutal because of my hair. I'm afraid to wear it in its naturally curly state or in braids for fear of judgment. I'm convinced that it will impact my career negatively. Reflecting on it saddens and frustrates me.

Getting ready for work takes an hour and fifteen minutes because my thick hair doesn't blow dry quickly, and then I straighten it with a flat iron. I'm frying my hair to make it look professional and attractive as deemed by society norms. About six months into my routine, I'm over it. Time to do what Black women call TBC, The Big Chop. I'll cut off all my processed hair (permanently relaxed/straightened with harmful chemicals) leaving only the naturally curly, coily, or kinky strands.

I arrive at the salon and tell my stylist, "Cut all my relaxed hair off." She's hesitant. "You sure, Tash?" But I confirm, "Let's do it!" I don't realize until after the cut that she doesn't have experience working with unrelaxed hair. Putting the scissors down, she says, "What do you want to do with it?" I look up at her incredulously. *Um... I'm here so you can help me figure that out! I have no idea what to do!* Expecting to see my curls come to life, I suggest, "Wet it and put some gel on it, I guess." Looking into the mirror, I panic at the sight of my new look. *I'm going to my first golf lesson looking a mess.* Holding back tears, I walk out, pretending I like the style.

It's too late to cancel my lesson without being charged. Although I'm embarrassed to be in public like this, I go anyway. I stop at Target on my way home to buy curly hair styling products and pray they'll create a miracle. Jumping in the shower as soon as I get back, I wash my hair and start experimenting. Goal: look presentable. I wonder what my colleagues will say while I consider calling in sick so I can take a day to figure out what to do. *What the hell was I thinking?*

I get up early and create some coils by applying tons of gel and wrapping small sections of hair around my finger. *Hmm, doesn't look that bad.* Hanging my head during the walking part of my commute, I'm self-conscious and convinced I look unattractive. Well, lo and behold, something totally unexpected happens: fellas started checkin' for me! Seriously, y'all! It's rare for people who aren't tourists to say hello in Washington, DC. But on *that* day? *Three* handsome men smile and greet me as we cross paths. *What!* Cheesin' commences. I'm still a single lady at this point, so uh ruh uh... they done put a li'l pep in this sista's step! I enter the office with my chin up and back straight, ready to take on the day.

Only a couple folks comment on it, but so many are looking at my hair. You know how you're making eye contact with a person, and their eyes are positioned to look at something other than yours? Yeah... that all day. I assume people don't like my new look, but still reveling in the attention from this morning, I shrug it off. The next day, when I'm ready for work just thirty minutes after my run, I know I made the right decision and don't care what anyone else thinks of it. The other good news? Compliments aren't uncommon once I embrace my hair, learning to style and care for it in its natural state.

About five years later, I travel to a leadership meeting in Fort Worth, Texas sporting a pineapple updo (if you're unfamiliar, search for photos online). I'm surprised to hear my name called as the winner of the Teamwork Award. I join the chief operating officer on the stage, shake her hand, and pose for a photo. She leans in and says, "Tash, I absolutely love your hair like that!" Water wells up in my eyes.

Five years into my natural hair journey, the beauty of me and my coils as they naturally grow from my head is recognized. Many outside of the Black community aren't aware of the trauma that Black women endure related to our hair—I talk to her about it later and she confirms she had no idea. I'm shocked and validated at the same time. More importantly, I'm proud of my decision to show up in a way I believe is beautiful because I know it makes room for others to do the same. Embracing myself as I am, big hair and all, helps me appreciate my uniqueness. I've grown the confidence to present myself as I want to, unapologetically. It's been more than twelve years since TBC, and the only regret I have is not doing it sooner.

If you're like me and want to change your appearance but don't because you worry what others will think, give yourself permission. One of my colleagues did just that. Todd Ruymen is well known for not only his expertise as an engineer but his unique and unconventional style. He's fly, y'all! What's so interesting is many of us can't wait to see what Ruymen's wearing every day—whether on Zoom or in person. On those days when Todd sports a more classic look, folks comment on that too. "Todd, looks like you're wearing a black jacket today. What's going on?" The group laughs, including Todd. "I'm a little toned down, but don't worry, I'll be back in something colorful tomorrow!"

"If you'd asked me in late high school or early college, I would have said there was no such thing as being authentic. I had to fit in and do exactly what everyone else was doing." Ruymen went to college planning to be an engineer but quickly recognized, even though he's a "numbers guy," he didn't enjoy the field of study. "I flipped completely and earned a degree in advertising. It really opened me up to understanding different cultures, different thought processes, and helped me realize I could be who I wanted to be."

Ruymen focused on building his credibility and developing relationships at work. "I pushed the envelope a little bit, established more credibility, and then pushed a little bit more. Sometimes, I pushed too far, but I learned from it and understand that balance is important." I agree, and having some balance helps us identify when there are some boundaries we have to work within. Ruymen says, "Live in the edges of the boundaries, and the more you establish your value, the more the boundaries are likely to widen."

In Chapter 5, "It's Not All About You," I pointed out people look to their supervisors to exemplify what's acceptable. "I had a manager who dressed in very bright colors and had a style uniquely hers. I appreciated it. It helped me feel more comfortable coming into a management role.

"Seeing his boss show up authentically made it clear to Ruymen that he could too. He takes that same approach with his children, who see their dad in tank tops showing his tattoo sleeves, in a purple suit, and even a velvet blazer. While his son keeps it simple, his daughter leans toward eclectic. (Yaaasss! love it!) She wears unique glasses matching her outfits, fun bows in her hair, and big frilly skirts with leggings. "It makes me proud that my eleven-year-old daughter is creating her own space to fit into because she realizes she can. She knows she doesn't have to conform, and that makes me happy."

These days, Ruymen wears what he enjoys. "I want to feel comfortable wearing my pink suit with alligator shoes and wearing my black suit with a black tie. That's important." It's about being able to do the job, especially in a professional environment, and beating the perceptions associated with appearances." Ruymen encourages us to focus on "what you do and the contributions you make so you can beat perception with reality."

HOW YOU COMMUNICATE

When we think about communication, in my experiences we focus on what we say more than anything else. *How* we say it matters just as much. My favorite guide on effective personal and professional communication is *Fierce Conversations: Achieving Success at Work and in Life, One Conversation at a Time* by Susan Scott (2004). Practicing Scott's principles since 2015 has heightened my communication ability so much, my friends and colleagues come to me for counsel on conversations they need to have. I'm regarded as an expert in verbal communication, often sought to coach or mentor others who wish to improve. The concepts Scott shares are straightforward, and I can affirm that they *work* based on my experiences.

Scott defines fierce conversation as "one in which we come out from behind ourselves into the conversation and make it real" (Scott 2004, 7). Love, love, love. The definition aligns with living authentically and being vulnerable—a key to being fiercely joyful. Scott highlights that relationships and careers are shaped one conversation at a time, explaining the conversation *is* our relationship (2004, 5). I'm a believer! I've built many important and enduring relationships with this understanding in mind. Here's the substance of Scott's concept.

THE 7 PRINCIPLES OF FIERCE CONVERSATIONS:

1. **Have the Courage to Investigate Reality**—one of my former managers always said there are three sides to every story: yours, mine, and the truth, which is usually somewhere in the middle. We must be willing to question our version of reality because it is influenced by our individual perspectives.
2. **Stop Hiding and Start Getting Real**—this starts with us being real with ourselves. Once we know and acknowledge our authentic self, we're better positioned to be vulnerable with others. It establishes trust.
3. **Be Here and Nowhere Else**—Being present means being engaged. Suspend distractions (put down our phones, ignore watch notifications, quiet our minds, etc.) and focus on the conversation.

4. **Confront Your Toughest Challenge Now**—It ain't gettin' easier with time, y'all. It's our responsibility to address issues when they arise to avoid the situation worsening.

5. **Follow Your Instincts**—Sometimes, a gut check will reveal answers we seek. We can tune in to what we're feeling on the inside for guidance. The tools in Chapter 4: Get Connected will be useful here.

6. **Take Responsibility for Your Emotional Wake**—What we say and do impacts others—either positively or negatively. Ideally, we minimize negative emotional wake but when it happens, we gotta own it.

7. **Use Silence Purposefully**—I love to talk! Being so vocal limits opportunities for others to weigh in, so remember to take a pause to let others speak or reflect a moment on what we've heard. Practice getting comfortable with silence, too. Think of it like white space—it's an opportunity to draw out insights.

The primary reason Scott's approach works for me is my acceptance of personal accountability in communications. In other words, looking inward is important to overcoming communication challenges. When I'm communicating, my intention is crystal clear to me, but is it to others? Did I choose words that reflect my intention accurately? Now, I cannot say I follow all seven principles all the time. What I keep in mind is this quote from Scott: "While no single conversation is *guaranteed* to change the trajectory of a career, a company, a relationship, or a life—any single conversation *can*" (Scott 2004, 157). It's happened to me at least a few times, so I'm vouching for Scott's assertion!

KEYS TO BEING FIERCELY JOYFUL:

"Owning your dopeness is not about being liked by others. It's really about being liked by you first. One of my favorite proverbs is: 'When there is no enemy within, the enemy outside can do you no harm.' If you are strong in yourself, the actions of everyone else are less likely to move you."

—LUVVIE AJAYI JONES, *PROFESSIONAL*
TROUBLEMAKER: THE FEAR-FIGHTER MANUAL

So what are the guardrails? The answer is, of course, it depends. Take Mom's experience and embrace it. Read your audience, ask your manager if you're not sure, and maybe test the waters a little bit at a time. What you shouldn't do is show up to work in sweats or booty shorts if you work at a law firm.

We all judge people by how they present. Yes, you too. It's in our nature. Why not make your first impression a great one before you even say a word? Let's face it, you're gonna win them over once you start talking, right? Score some bonus points upfront.

🔑 **Learn what makes you confident in your appearance.** Identify your style—what makes you feel good, not what everyone else likes. Consider your body type, colors you love, fabric, and any other requirements you have. Post-COVID-19, I won't buy anything that doesn't stretch, is loose fitting—and buttons or zippers on my pants are prohibited. Now it's pull-on pants with hidden elastic waist, baby! If this sounds like a different language, find a style consultant to help—either one you pay or one of your friends whose look you admire.

- **Evaluate your environment.** Particularly at work, dress appropriately for the setting. Find out if there's an official dress code. If not, look around and take note of what you see. And, don't be afraid to ask. Talk to your manager to address your questions, give specific examples (e.g., "I see everyone here wears suits. Is it okay to wear sneakers with mine? How about a blazer and cargo pants?") and get feedback.

- **Make eye contact.** When you're the one talking, look folks in the eye. Notice that I said "folks," which is plural. If several people are in your discussion or meeting, avoid turning it into a one-on-one conversation. Keep others engaged by making eye contact with the group as a whole, as well as with the person your words are directed to. Now, you've created an unspoken invitation encouraging others to speak up, which demonstrates you value the participation of *everyone* in the room.

- **Be mindful.** Remember *how* you say what you say is important. Take a moment to formulate your message or even practice in advance. And, *how* you act—that gravitas (one more shoulder shake) is an opportunity to be well-received from the start.

Now hear this: be polished, but be *you!* Luckily, this is no longer the 1980s, so you can be polished in a way that's authentically you. For me, that looks like my naturally curly hair (read: *big* hair, don't care), a diamond nose stud, and threads that feel good on my skin—classy with a li'l bit of edge. Sometimes, I combine unexpected colors and textures or break out statement jewelry that carries the look. Again, it's all about what feels good. Go ahead and polish yo'self.

10

MOVE YOUR BODY AND EASE YOUR MIND

"Exercise is not only a key to physical health but to peace of mind."

—NELSON MANDELA

As a preteen, clothes shopping is traumatic for me because I've always had body issues. I'm way taller than average for my age at five feet, eight inches, and I'm what Black people refer to as big-boned. We use the term as a nice way (sort of) of saying "fat but not too fat." Many years later, I recognize my bones actually *are* large compared to the average woman. For example, there is I have no fat around my wrists, even today, but I have to buy a large-sized or adjustable bracelet. When I look at pictures of my preteen and teenage self, I'm actually skinny!

My tall, large frame and big bones makes it hard to find clothes, which means shopping in the special section for "husky" or "stocky" girls. My cheeks grow red, revealing my embarrassment when we walk to the back of the store to find my size clothing. Special sizes suck. I want a pair of Guess jeans like my friends have, but can't get them over my hips. I keep the image of big-boned me in mind for years to come—the fat kid who is different from everyone else.

I struggle with my weight off and on for my entire life, even now. As of this writing, my exercise is sporadic at best. I'm in the final stretch of revisions, which requires much more of a time investment than expected. Temporary stress and overwhelm are leading to poor sleep. I decide to recognize this moment as one ripe for giving myself grace.

Thank goodness I'm a healthy eater, which mitigates the typical ailments associated with being obese. Yep, I'm not just overweight. I'm obese. And this is after I had weight loss surgery (gastric bypass) several years ago. I lose over seventy pounds after the procedure and maintain it for over two years, then comes COVID. No, the vaccine doesn't make me gain weight, I make me gain weight. Due to work, I'm living in a different city than my husband, lonely, and afraid of what is to come from the disease, particularly over the first six to eight months. I stay indoors, stop exercising (my default is to walk or jog outdoors), and eat poorly.

Staying committed to being physically active comes easy for some, not all. Once I get in the habit, I enjoy the benefits of it, including the contentment and peace I experience by following through on self-care. I've learned to give myself some grace and compassion, steering away from setting unreasonable expectations. Now, I'm not off the hook. Holding myself accountable is important, too. It's simply a work-in-progress based on the current state of my life. I once participated in a month-long challenge designed to inspire regular exercise. The requirement was to work out for fifteen minutes, five days per week. Fifteen minutes? Of course, I can dedicate fifteen minutes to exercise! If you experience challenges like me, maybe you can start there too.

Speaking of creating habits, I recommend James Clear's book *Atomic Habits: Tiny Changes, Remarkable Results.* It's an easy read and an excellent resource on taking small steps that lead to meaningful change.

For a long time, I don't recognize the connection between physical and mental wellness. The importance of the connection is undeniable! I am at my very best when I commit to and follow through on caring for myself holistically. Read on for stories and strategies on how we can accomplish just that.

I WAS SEEN

Living in Southern Maryland, I have a long commute to work in Washington, DC. The volume of traffic means three hours of driving daily. The stress of it took a toll on me, so I transition to the taking the bus, using commuting time to read, catch up on email, or even nap. I'm anxious my first time on the bus. *Can I walk the aisle without my hips bumping everyone I pass? What if I have to share and I'm in the aisle seat?* I avoid the hip bumps by twisting my body while walking. When I find a seat, it's on the aisle. My right hip is squashed against the immobile armrest and on top of a blunt steel lever used to adjust the seat back. It's painful, but since I'm embarrassed, I hide it. I'm frozen, unwilling to move for fear of greater pain, while looking around wondering if anyone is watching and judging me.

My mind races, formulating a plan for getting out of the seat without making a scene. *If I use the seat in front of me to extract myself, the weight I put on it will disturb the passenger in it.* I act like everything is normal until I get to my stop. This is the beginning of years of anxiety all related to my weight.

I buy tickets for me and Edwaun to see the Alvin Ailey Dance Theatre perform at the Kennedy Center. A week before the show, I panic, wondering if I'll fit into the seat. Despite hours scouring the internet looking for measurements of the theatre seats, I'm unsuccessful. I don't want to call and ask. I'm too ashamed. With the anxiety worsening as the event nears, I consider pretending I'm sick to avoid going.

Saturday arrives; I push past overwhelming unease and get dressed. Hands trembling, I abandon lip liner, swipe on clear gloss, and tell myself, *It's gonna be fine.* In the theatre, I'm unable to sit in the seat as one normally would because my hips are too wide. Instead, I sit on the edge and then slide back into the seat; my waist being two sizes smaller than my hips makes this feasible. *Thank you, heavenly Father!* My thighs spill out beyond the surface of the seat, but no one easily sees it. Exhaling, I hear the music begin, and I'm grateful to watch the show.

I become obsessed with how my obese body will impact the things I want to do. On the bus, I plan and replay again and again in my head how I will get up if I have to let someone out to get off before my stop—getting out of the seat is hard when you're obese. I never accept a booth at a restaurant because I draw attention getting in and out of one. I only drive SUVs because seatbelts in sedans nearly choke me, and feeling my head graze the roof of the car makes me claustrophobic. Before committing to going anywhere, I factor in my obesity. It takes a toll, and depression kicks in on top of the anxiety.

One day, a colleague I don't know well invites me into her office. "How are you doing?" I lie. "Fine thanks, and you?" Leaning toward me, she suggests, "You don't seem like yourself." Breaking eye contact, I worry she's "caught" me pretending to be okay. I learn later she recognizes in my eyes what she experienced herself. How I go from pretend happy to an ugly cry is somewhat of a blur. Puddles form on my lap, kicking off a firehose-style confessional of the hurt and sadness I've been holding inside. My colleague shares she's dealt with depression, sought treatment, and found her way through it. "I know you can too, Tash."

Being *seen* provides some relief, my heart warmed by the care of a colleague I barely know. She doesn't hesitate to be vulnerable despite not knowing how I would react or if I'd put her business in the street. How lucky am I that she chose to support me rather than protect herself? She encourages me to seek help. "Depression and anxiety are medical conditions for which there are treatments. See your doctor like you would for any medical concern." I call my doctor the next day.

For at least twenty years, I battled lengthy periods of anxiety and depression, suffering silently. I am beyond grateful for my colleague showing me such compassion. She could have handled the situation in so many other ways. She chose the selfless and kind option, which is why she is now a friend. Guess what? Her actions helped change my life for the better. I finally got help and recognized I'm not alone. I embrace talking openly about my struggles, practice prioritizing my health, and take care of me in a whole new way. Though I still have challenges at times, I now know what I'm capable of. I recognize the symptoms of a problem. I no longer put myself at the bottom of the to-do list. I choose me.

CHOOSE HEALTH

"Health and fitness is a lifestyle, not a hobby," shares Robin Marion, Founder and CEO of Velvet & Steel Fitness, LLC, an ACE certified personal trainer, ACE certified health coach, and nutrition coach. "My philosophy is to be proactive about my health. We shouldn't wait for something to go wrong and then promise to change. We already know better, so why not do better now?" Marion, army first sergeant (retired), disliked physical fitness in the military because it was a job requirement, not an activity she was taught the importance of in terms of having a better quality of life. "When I was exposed to people benefiting from taking better control of their health, I looked at physical fitness differently and recognized the value it brings."

Growing up a kid on the South Side of Chicago, Marion had a strong desire to play sports, yet wasn't permitted to do so. She was raised by her grandmother and kept under her wing. Determined to find a way, she joined her high school's volleyball, basketball, and track teams, unbeknownst to her family. "I told my grandmother I was in after-school activities when I was at practice. I hid my involvement in sports for three years." Hearing this, I wanted to understand how this impacted Marion's authenticity. "I resented not being able to just be me and do what made me happy. As a teenager, I had more responsibility than some adults do. Athletics was a way to escape challenges at home and feel happy."

Recognizing her family wasn't taught the importance of being physically active and taking care of themselves, Marion understands why it wasn't a focus in her rearing. "I made a commitment to talk to my kids about their health and encourage movement so they have a foundation upon which to build with their own families down the road. When they asked, 'Why do I have to eat broccoli?' my answer wasn't 'Because I said so.' I explained the nutritional benefits to their body and mind."

Marion's kids have embraced fitness as a lifestyle; both are award-winning athletes, just like their mom and dad. Even in their fifties, Marion and her husband compete in and have won numerous figure competitions. "My philosophy to a healthy lifestyle is fitness, and health is a journey. There are no quick fixes, only hard work, determination, consistency, and honesty. Transformation starts with the mind, and the body will follow."

I'm a huge advocate for seeking professional help in support of your health and fitness journey. Marion and I became friends more than a decade ago when beginning our amateur running careers. I've been one of her clients too. She's highly qualified with more than a dozen certifications. I appreciate her credentials in both physical and nutritional health, enabling her to provide comprehensive services to clients often pressed for time. Marion's commitment to helping others achieve their goals is unwavering.

Flexibility is critical. I texted, "Burpees are damn near impossible for me. Can you give me something to replace them in my workout?" Marion responds, "Absolutely! I'll send some options." You'll want someone who holds you accountable yet understands you don't need to be kicked when you're already down. She helps clients look at why they've had setbacks and how to overcome them. My client relationship with Marion was a partnership and led to me achieving my objectives. If you hire a professional, consider these qualifications during your search.

My colleague, friend, and accountability coach, Nick Fuller, a federal government executive, prioritizes health and fitness. "I'm unwilling to compromise my physical fitness." Fuller practices jiujitsu and is a medaled competitor. He's competitive by nature and values success, which pushes him to be his best in all aspects of life. Once, I had the nerve to challenge him to a seven-day Apple Fitness competition. Now, if it was a period of time when I was working out more often, I mighta still lost, but not so terribly. He pummeled me every day. Morning cardio workout, morning walk, afternoon walk, evening strength training, evening walk. "I don't have a TV to entertain me, so I'm exploring my neighborhood instead." All I know is, I took one hell of a beatin'! He's since invested in a big TV yet still accumulates three to five workouts daily. Hmph. #Envious

Fuller's family is from the South (Louisiana and Georgia). If you're even the tiniest bit health conscious, you're probably raising your brows. The South is well known for amazing cuisine. There are rich traditions around food in every culture. For Southerners, particularly Black people, it's soul food. Soul food typically means fried foods, often the unhealthiest part of animal products (the fattiest parts, which yield great flavor), and sweet desserts like pie and pound cake.

Vegetables are usually cooked for extensive amounts of time, resulting in a loss of nutritional value. In Black culture, we historically overcook foods, and I'm guilty of it to this day. If my scrambled eggs aren't a li'l browned, they're not done. Bacon must be crispy, and when I used to eat steak, I ordered it well-done. I know some of y'all are gasping at the thought of well-done meat! I do have plenty of Black friends who refuse a well-done steak; again, no community is a monolith, but for my brother Ellis and my husband? Well-done is a must.

I would be remiss if I didn't address how the soul food tradition began. Black people's diets were influenced by slavery. Slaves got scraps their owners refused to eat. When you have something with no flavor, what do you do? You find ways to make it taste good, like fry it in fatback. In today's world, writer Jazz Keyes states, "[R]acial disparities influence the overall physical health of Blacks in America. African Americans, specifically those who live in low-income neighborhoods of lower socio-economic status, have less access to quality foods and sufficient healthcare" (Keyes 2019).

"I wasn't raised to tend to my health. Some of my family members had poor eating habits and didn't focus on physical activity. Those were big factors in their longevity, which was lacking." What Fuller saw in his family is common in my experiences. On the other hand, some of his family spent time in the military. There was a very clear delineation in the healthiness of those families. They focused on physical fitness and eating healthy—and had longer lifespans. "One of my aunts who embraced the military influence is in her seventies and hikes every single day. She hiked through Germany once. When I visit her, we walk around town, do winery tours, and have a blast."

Fuller is a navy veteran with an appreciation for the military lifestyle related to health and fitness. "Being physically fit, I love being able to do physically challenging things for a prolonged period of time, and really enjoy it. It's like the difference between seeing things from the deck of a cruise ship versus actually being out there and experiencing it myself." Though you won't catch him lying on a beach in Maui for ten days straight, you'll certainly see Fuller in a selfie at the top of a mountain overlooking the city—likely a mountain not many traverse (did I mention his competitive spirit?).

When he used to take his daughter to soccer practice, Fuller jogged around the field while the kids played. The other parents told him they didn't understand why he did it. "It was the perfect time for me to get in my exercise while also enjoying watching my daughter practice. When you become a parent, you don't have to give up everything you love. You just have to be creative about finding another way to do it." His daughter saw his example and picked up the same healthy habits, which makes Fuller happy because he sees her balancing the important things in life. I appreciate Nick's perspective on this because where there's a will, there's a way.

PERFECT AIN'T NECESSARY, CONSISTENCY IS KEY
It's no secret the exercise train is one folks often fall off, and getting back on can be sooooo hard, especially if

you're not a morning person who can make it happen at the start of the day before interruptions surface (read: no excuses prevent you from doing it first but if you plan to do it last, there are lots of excuses to choose from).

There is lots of research about what time of day is best for exercise. An article in *The Washington Post* cites a recent study concluding, "Afternoon exercise may reduce the risks of premature death more than morning or evening workouts, according to a new large-scale study of more 90,000 men and women." On the other hand, the same article states, "if you'd like to burn a little more fat with each workout and slowly lower your body's fat stores, there may be advantages to exercising before noon" (Reynolds 2023).

Sounds like we can benefit from moving regardless of the time we choose. We can certainly leverage research to inform our decisions, though ultimately, do what works best for you. What can you commit to logistically, based on your overall schedule? Habits stick when you can reasonably execute them, *and* you've bought into them unequivocally.

Fuller suggests, "Set specific goals and avoid focusing so much on the end game" (for help with this read on to Chapter 13: Embrace the Journey). "You need to *just start* with a goal comfortable for you, not what anyone else is pushing you to do, and build on it over time." In my own experiences, incremental progress with realistic goals leads to success for me. "Focus on achieving some success, and once you start seeing successes accumulate, you'll be motivated to keep going until it becomes a habit. After a few months, it becomes part of your lifestyle. You'll learn to be less discouraged when you don't hit a certain goal, than when you miss out on investing in yourself."

After years of repeating the behavior, it was a lightbulb moment when I realized my habit of completely giving up when I fell off the wagon. I held myself to an unreasonable standard of never missing a planned workout or never straying from my meal plan. Bottom line? *I was the barrier to my success.* Not allowing myself the grace to fail a little resulted in me failing myself completely. If you've found yourself operating in a similar all-or-nothing mindset, here's an opportunity to evolve. Whether it's been two days since I've eaten a vegetable or two months, nothing stops me from some sautéed spinach today—same for you! Any moment is a good one to try again.

FITNESS AIN'T JUST PHYSICAL

My story about being seen illustrates how important holistic fitness is to our health. I was consumed by the anxiety I experienced from being obese. Marion sees emotional, mental, and spiritual wellness directly connected to physical health. "When we're not functioning well in one or more of these areas, it may impact our physical fitness. Stress, emotional challenges, or a lack of spiritual balance can make it difficult to be fully present or committed to physical fitness." At the same time, she shares that regular physical activity can help reset your emotional, mental, or spiritual wellness. "We all have times when we're out of balance—it happens throughout life. The important thing to remember is the interconnectivity exists, so we have to nurture ourselves fully."

"All stress, anxiety, depression, is caused when we ignore who we are, and start living to please others."
—PAULO COELHO, AUTHOR OF *THE ALCHEMIST*

Let me call attention to authenticity in relation to being holistically fit. Showing up in ways not true to yourself can be damaging mentally and physically. Marion reflects, "For a long time, I tried so much to please everybody else, and it caused me so much physical and emotional stress. I decided I'm not going to do this anymore. A weight lifted off me; it felt like freedom." She embraces meditation and prayer to ease day-to-day stress.

In a conversation with an acquaintance serving in the role of president and CEO for her employer, she remarked, "I constantly have to tamp down my emotions at work. It's exhausting, but I have to do it." Welp, I see it differently, "You *have* to? Why?" Her response, "The bulk of my employees are men. They judge me if I get emotional."

"I understand and want to offer a few thoughts for your consideration. First, if you find yourself frequently censoring your truth, are you showing up authentically? Second, if the president and CEO can't normalize a productive and honest show of emotion in the workplace, who can? Last, it seems you have a choice here rather than a requirement. The choice might be an uncomfortable one to make, yet you have the power to do it." My remark about authenticity resonated strongly with her. "Wow, I hadn't thought about compromising my authenticity by holding back. Thank you. I'm going to reflect on how I make a change."

When leaders show emotion at work, it's a sign of strength, not weakness. How can being true to your feelings be weak? You're being authentic, which takes courage. Don't let anyone convince you otherwise. Your emotions do need to be managed, yet they can be displayed productively.

When I ask Fuller what he wishes he knew sooner, he says, "I wish I better understood the importance of mental and emotional fitness." As I've often heard men say, he wasn't encouraged or even taught how to deal with his emotions. Honestly, how many of us are taught how to manage our emotions? The bulk of my learning has come from my mistakes. If I recognized sooner this is a learned skill, perhaps I could have avoided a few mistakes.

It's been said we're in a mental health crisis across the country. I turn on the news and learn about heightened numbers of suicides, particularly in younger age groups. People around us are sometimes suffering, and we don't even realize it. Because so many well-known people are being open about their challenges with mental health, it seems the stigma is beginning to break down. A newly elected senator publicly announced he was checking himself into the hospital for severe depression. Such transparency has been unheard of up until now.

What I want you to understand is what my doctor told me when I realized I was suffering from anxiety and depression: these are medical conditions requiring attention and perhaps treatment just like any other health concern. It could be mild or serious, which is why it's important to seek professional treatment. Don't minimize it to a few bad days when you've been suffering for months. If loved ones brush it off, either push back or go do you. Would you overlook chest pains? Cloudy vision? Numbness or tingling in your limbs? The answer is no. Make your appointment and get help.

KEYS TO BEING FIERCELY JOYFUL:

- **Move to your beat.** If you don't already know what physical activities you enjoy, try some out. What you should not do is go sign up for an annual gym membership unless you are certain you can incorporate gym workouts into your routine habits. Start gradually if you're new to exercising, and make sure your doctor gives you a thumbs up first. I used to be a Zumba teacher—whether I was teaching class or participating as a student, it never felt like a chore because I love dancing. I was motivated to go as often as I could. Your Zumba or running might be golf, swimming, kickboxing, walking, cycling—explore and find out.
- **Eat to live.** If you're a not-so-healthy eater, talk to your doctor about what they recommend for you. You can find tons of information online about the best things and ways to eat, but everything online isn't accurate. Check with your doc before trying anything new, and you might want to talk to a nutritionist or

dietician as well. You can start small by reducing your sugar intake, replacing one soda or serving of juice with some good ol' H2O.

- **Listen to your body.** When something doesn't feel right, please don't ignore it. Better safe than sorry. See your physician and do a check in. Plan your annual checkups to coincide with your birthday month as a gift of self-care for yourself.

- **Prioritize holistic health.** Mind, body, and soul, y'all—it all matters. First, acknowledge where you are along your journey. Look for small steps you can take to improve where needed. Back in Chapter 4: Get Connected, the Keys to Being Fiercely Joyful can help here, too. If you have unreconciled trauma, look into support groups or counseling. Tons of resources are available, many for free, when you're ready to do the work.

11

YOUR TRUE CREW

"Lots of people want to ride with you in the limo, but what you want is someone who will take the bus with you when the limo breaks down."

—OPRAH WINFREY

A LESSON FROM DAD

My friend John has a heart of gold. We both go through tough times in the early 2000s, and he always has my back. I talk about John often, so Dad's looking forward to meeting him when he comes to visit. Since I live in Northern Virginia not far from Old Town Alexandria, we have dinner at the Chart House.

We drink wine while waiting to be seated. Dad and John hit it off. John, knowledgeable and funny, enters into engaging conversation with ease. I'd told him lots of my favorite stories about Dad. He's eager to talk to the man behind so many of the unforgettable experiences I'd shared.

Dad chats with other folks, too. He can never be accused of being antisocial. Being the kid of such a gregarious person is annoying at times. I'd want Dad all to myself only to hear him inviting someone we didn't know to join us for lunch. I don't grow to *accept* it, but I grow to *expect* it, so it's less annoying over time. There's a silver lining here. Watching Dad develop deep, meaningful friendships out of such ordinary encounters showed me how to build my own support system—my True Crew.

Chatting with a woman he just met, Dad says, "Let me introduce you to my kids. This is Tash, and this is John." She greets us with a smile but can't hide her puzzlement. Oh, wait... I didn't tell you. John is White. My skin is a little darker than John's, and Dad has deep brown melanin. With curiosity, she continues, "They're both your kids or John, are you his son-in-law?" Dad responds, "No, he's not my son-in-law. He's my son." She tries again. "Oh. So, is John adopted?" Now she done went too far, and Dad is not having it. "Listen, these are both my kids, okay? Period. So, tell me, what do you do for a living?" And that was the end of it.

I *love* how Dad handled that. I'm sure I would have answered all her questions and said, "Well, he's not really my brother, but he's like one." Dad's response is far better because why does it even matter? John loves it, too. Dad is unwilling to single him out as different. He's family and that's that. From that point on, John drops Mr. Craig and calls him Dad.

Fooling someone wasn't Dad's objective. He was unequivocal in recognizing we *choose* the family we're not born with, and we should cherish them just the same. Anyone important to his biological kids was important to him, too. Dad didn't care for labels. Family was family regardless of how it came to be and didn't need to be explained. I couldn't agree with him more.

Less than two years later, when Dad dies, John is the first to show up. He wrapped me in his arms only letting go after I did. Before he sits, John pulls from his pocket a piece of paper haphazardly snatched from a notebook. I get a closer look after he unfolds it and see scribbles I can't decipher. "Tash, I'm not exactly sure what to say, but I know there are some things we will need to do, so I've started a list." It was such an act of love and kindness. And that big ol' heart is why John is still part of my crew today.

Sometimes, my gut tells me to act, and though I often lack clarity on why I should, I still follow through. Since I've accepted that and grown used to it, I proceed anyway, quickly weighing any risk associated with it. If I decide it's a risk with consequences that I can tolerate, I move out.

One day, my gut (heretofore known as Sugie, Mom's nickname) tells to me to call someone I work with but barely know to share something uplifting. I met my associate Jessica in person just once and a few times on Zoom. In the same room together, her energy is sweet and invigorating. I knew I was meeting an amazing woman.

Soon after our in-person meeting, Sugie told me to call Jessica and share with her how I experienced her that day. *Really? I don't know this woman from Adam, and she'll think I'm strange if I call her up with such outlandishness.* Though hesitant, I make the call anyway. We finally connect a couple months later.

When doing what Sugie tells me to, I explain upfront, putting aside how unusual the circumstances, I've sensed a need to reach out to them. Jessica answers my call, I offer my disclaimer, and share meeting her was a wonderful experience. "I sensed your spirit with such powerful brightness akin to sunshine filling up a room. Your warmth drew me in, making me grateful to connect, even if only for a short time. I wanted you to know."

After a few moments of silence, I hear Jessica sniffing while saying she's navigating a difficult time and needed to hear my words. She carries a heavy load. Her children are sick—one is hospitalized as we speak. Jessica is a business owner and executive spread thin and focused on taking care of everyone except herself. Seeing similar behavior in ourselves is common, isn't it? Personally, I've mastered putting myself last. You too? Keep reading, and you'll learn how to kick the habit.

Jessica shares she's overwhelmed and exhausted. She spends her day following through on a multitude of commitments and at night cries in her bedroom. I tell Jessica I know she has a strong support system—amazing people always do. We volunteer happily to help the most awesome people we know. "Why aren't you calling on them?" Jessica worries about burdening others.

Now, I need to move from comforting to Gentle Bully (a nickname my coworkers gave me). I remind Jessica that her crew *wants* to help. I tell her to start with taking one task off her plate. Ask a crew member to drop off dinner, pick up her child from school or practice, grab a few things from the grocery store, or simply pick up her dry cleaning. Whatever is helpful, she needs to *ask* and *let* folks step in. Think about it. We all have that small group of loved ones whom we support at the drop of a dime—we're on the sideline in uniform waiting to be called into the game. Yet, we rarely get the call. So pick up the phone, send a text, or show up at their house. They're ready and happy to help.

We inflict pain, frustration, and more on ourselves by walking around like superhumans. *Please* stop it. Recognize this approach to life can turn toxic. I've been there, holding everything inside and pretending I'm okay when I'm not. That can devastate our mental health. It can even result in physical health problems like stress-induced headaches or worse. Together, let's take a healthier approach. Give yourself permission to accept help. You hold the power to avoid self-inflicted harm by calling on your crew. Your crew is your support system. They're your chosen family.

Now, let me be clear about something: *everyone willing should* not *be hired.* Just because somebody is applying for membership on your crew, doesn't require you to approve their application. Chile', there will be folks *pressed* to get the job, yet you're not interested in offering them the position. Guess what? There is *nuthin'* wrong with that. Be friends or acquaintances, if you desire, but don't succumb to pressure or feel guilty if they're not a fit for your crew. Remember, this is your fiercely joyful quest. What *you* want matters. Be comfortable with your choice and cultivate only those crew relationships right for you.

TWO KINDS OF CREWS

The crew that *everyone* must have is your *True Crew.* They have your back as you traverse the ups and downs of life—your True Crew softens the landing when you fall and celebrates you for being you. Your True Crew is an important part of your fiercely joyful life because connectedness with the right people helps us thrive. The other crew that I strongly recommend is a *Community Crew.* A sense of community feeds your soul and help fills your cup.

True Crew members are ready to support you, anytime and anywhere. Think of them as ride or die as long as it's not in a toxic sense. Some boundaries are a must. It's not about extreme friendship where someone will make choices to be there for you in ways that have awful consequences. No burying bodies. (Uh huh... I know somebody reading this is thinking, *Well, why not?* Cuz y'all will ruin your lives and go to jail, that's why. And because it's just not a good thing to take folks out. Moving on.) True Crew supports you in healthy and compassionate ways. They know you well. I mean they *know* you... sometimes better than you know yourself, skeletons and all. You can attempt to fool your True Crew, but you never succeed (a la, "Yeah, I'm doing good" when you're really not). You've been friends with some members for decades, some might be family and others are newer friends, quickly proven invaluable.

You *always* get to be *you* in *all ways* with your True Crew. You're welcomed *just as you are*! They love you. All of you. No modulating or walking on eggshells. You get to be fully you without restrictions. Whew! Just thinking about the freedom of being me makes me smile!

TRUE CREW MEMBERSHIP

Let me be clear. I am *not* telling you to issue a vacancy announcement for True Crew members, okay? What *I am saying* is have clarity about what you can expect from your crew. It's not uncommon for one True Crew member to fill more than one role on a regular basis. If you feel like a role is vacant, you can ask one of your members to fill in from time to time. Heaven knows, any True Crew member worth their salt will try their best. Here's what you need from your True Crew:

- Comes to your aid without question. As long as it's not illegal or unethical (well... the latter is a maybe because it might depend), this person will not ask thirteen questions about why you need what you need. They will just do what you need. Like drive forty-five minutes to pick you up and take you home after you had one too many shots, old-fashioneds, margaritas... you get my point.
- You haven't talked to them in months, sometimes years, but it feels like no time is lost when you reunite. You don't have to offer your first-born child in penance for not calling or texting. They're thrilled to talk to or spend time with you.
- They always tell you the truth, particularly truths you don't want to hear. Now, you two may disagree, and you may decide not to take their advice, but this friend won't hold that against you for a second; they'll support you either way. Note: They may be petty if it turns out you should have listened to them, but they'll just say, "I told you" (if we're always right, we just *have* to say it) and then move on.
- A friend listens and empathizes without trying to fix the problem. Sometimes you just need to vent, cry, or cuss. Whatever it is, they're there for it. They entertain your daydreams about the mean things you want to but will never do... like maybe stick your foot out and trip somebody you can't stand, accidentally of course.
- They remind you of your courage when fear gets in the way of opportunity. They look at you sideways when you lay out reasons you can't do something

that they know you can absolutely do. Kind of like a cheerleader but not in an obnoxious way.

- Your stronghold friend is impeccable with their word, especially related to follow-through. If you ask them to do something for you by a certain date, it's typically done early... and they might actually worry you with questions because they're going to make sure they deliver *exactly* what you need. We may roll our eyes at all those dang questions, but we totally love their worried, perfectionist self.

- They hold you accountable. They might ask questions they already know the answer to like, "How were your workouts this week?" knowing damn well they haven't gotten any notifications from Apple Watch Fitness app about you burning a single active calorie. Despite that, somebody has to hold our feet to the fire when we don't do it ourselves.

- All True Crew Members not only accept you as you are, they encourage you to be you and won't accept anything else.

COMMUNITY CREWS

We're on a family vacation in Hawaii. The luau—a Hawaiian feast—made me reminisce on our family reunions, albeit the weather was never as beautiful. My hips swing to lively music unlike any I'd heard before as I mimic the moves of women wearing grass skirts. During a slow twirl, I freeze when I see it. A *whole entire pig* is cooking on a rotisserie spinning at a snail's pace. I've never seen an entire animal—literally head to toe—being cooked! *I'm* so *not eating that.* "Mom, I've never eating pork again. Do you see the pig's head?" She nods and hits me with a conundrum. "So you're giving up bacon then, your favorite?" *On second thought, I'm not giving up bacon.*

The luau is Dad's favorite part of the trip. He loves the sense of connectedness that he experiences. So, of course, when we get home, Dad plans our very own pig roast. Hundreds are invited from across Scranton and neighboring cities. My older brothers (Dad's sons) live in Harrisburg, Pennsylvania, with their mom and always come to the pig roasts. We treat pig roasts like holidays, and I love that the whole family is together.

Our entire home is made for entertaining. In the backyard, the covered patio with built-in tables along the perimeter is where everyone likes to chill. The oval-shaped underground pool is nine feet on the deep end and three feet in the shallow. Tucked in the corner away from the pool is the outdoor brick oven and grill Dad used for slow-cooking meats. On the other side is the pool house that stores pool toys and the equipment to clean it, one of the chores Ellis and I share.

The basement is designed for dining, drinking, and dancing. Eight round tables made from the wood spindles Dad got for free from the cable company fill the room. He covered the spines with carpet remnants and the tops with red and black leather attached with brass nailheads. We have a full bar. Behind it and in the back of the basement are walls of tiled mirrors splashed with red paint. The rest of the walls are painted black with silver streaks. A long lacquered red buffet table spans the entire back wall. The thick shag carpet is various colors of gray. The front part of the basement is the dance floor. No obstructions, just a big round disco light on the ceiling and space for you to get your groove on!

Mom prepares food for days ahead of time. I'm her helper. She's exhausted and questioning her husband's judgment for wanting to have the pig roast in the first place. When the special day finally arrives, food is everywhere—just about everything you could imagine. An array of hors d'oeuvres, cheese, shrimp cocktail, macaroni and cheese, potato salad, fruits, fried fish, chicken, other meats, desserts, and so much more. Once everything is ready and the gate to the backyard opens, one glance reveals this extravaganza is a labor of love.

The Craigs' Pig Roast is held in the summer—usually July or August. Every year, I'm giddy looking around and seeing people streaming in all day and evening while music plays in the background. Their expressions show they're having fun. Tons of laughter, kids playing, new friendships blossoming, and old ones being nurtured. Inside is more of the same, plus dancing.

Experiences like our pig roasts taught me the importance of being in community with others. Dad always thought it best to do so while breaking bread. Think about it... when surrounded by great food, aren't you a bit disarmed? A little less guarded? I saw Dad mend fences, have tough conversations, share appreciation, and simply rejoice in the present moment, all in the presence of food. To this day, bringing people together brings me joy, and I know that comes from Dad.

We have so much to gain from being in community with others, whether it's our neighbors, alumni circle, a faith-based group, professional network, etc. Experiences driven by commonality lead to a sense of belonging, connectedness, personal growth, and even establishing support networks. This outside your comfort zone? Ask yourself what you have to lose by trying. Find a community group that interests you and show up. Commit to staying for twenty minutes, and if you're not feeling it, leave. If the people and discussion resonate, stick with it and enjoy.

I'm honored to interview Melissa Proctor, author of *From Ball Girl to CMO* and the chief marketing officer for the Atlanta Hawks to gain insights for this book. "Do your relationships play a role in how you show up?" Proctor affirms relationships are important, and at work, both management and peers can provide support and empowerment.

In her personal life, Proctor seeks out people with shared interests, or are part of the groups she connects with. You have control over how you spend your time outside of work, so you should "go where acceptance is," she says. Proctor loves the book by Matthew W. Ragas and Bolivar J. Bueno called *The Power of Cult Branding* (2002, 3). "It talks about the Maslow's Hierarchy of Needs and the idea of self-actualization. You might connect with fans of Oprah or Jimmy Buffett. Maybe you connect with

Harley Davidson owners or wrestling fanatics. You are part of those crews. People who love *Star Wars*, like it's so deep... *Star Trek* Trekkies, they connect to each other by connecting around whatever unites them. I think that's beautiful."

Thinking about Proctor's point, I have several crews that relate to things I enjoy. I have a run crew, a fashion crew, a social and political issues crew, my work crew, and probably a few more. It's a wonderful thing to be able to fit into multiple spaces. If you have interests spanning more than one area, and crews to go along with them, that may be an indicator of a fulfilling life. On the other hand, don't break your neck trying to keep up with 101 crews, okay? Even though I do have several, I'm not active in all of them at the same time. Be careful not to spread yourself too thin. Balance, as always, is key. That means you might have to prioritize one crew over another when they're both active at the same time. Guess what? That's fine. Choose what feels right to you in the moment (refer to Chapter 4: Get Connected for tactics on identifying what your gut is telling you).

CREW MAINTENANCE

One of my crew members is Demetre Downing (who I call Dee). We meet in 1997 when I move with my then fiancé and now ex-husband to the Atlanta area from Washington, DC. Dee and I work for a software company in entry-level positions. Being from Scranton, Pennsylvania, where we greet one another and know all our neighbors, I go about getting to know my new coworker. I know right away that she's special—I feel it in my gut. Dee has a hard exterior, but I sense her inner teddy bear despite her efforts to hide it.

Now, she and I tell the story of how our friendship blossomed quite differently. I interviewed her for this book so I could share her *inaccurate* version based on an assumption that I am simply nosy. Dee wonders why in the hell I keep talking to her day after day and trying to get into her business. My version, the accurate one—lol—is I have an intuition about her. Although I don't know why, I know we need to connect. We are complete opposites, and I'm sure that's why we became friends. Whew, she was a tough nut to crack though!

Dee has a Georgia accent and a beautiful smile. When I ask personal questions, she looks at me sideways and says, "Why do you want to know?" wondering about my motive. So used to someone having an ulterior motive, she assumes the same of me. I share as much as I ask and too much for her taste. "Is there anything you keep to yourself?" That's how she realizes over time, I'm just being me. No strings attached.

She feels judged often, leading her to conform to others' idea of her instead of her own. Eventually, she doesn't know anymore the woman *she* wants to be. I ask questions about her dreams, and I'm interested in her perspectives on everything. I welcome Dee into my life exactly as she is in that moment. I don't want her to be anything else because I love how she shows up.

Dee and I have been through hell and back together dealing with life issues that run the gambit: significant loss and the resulting grief, professional crises, relationship challenges, mental and emotional health breakdowns... and an extended period of time when we were disconnected.

"Growing apart doesn't change the fact that for a long time we grew side by side; our roots will always be tangled. I'm glad for that."

—ALLY CONDIE

DISAPPEARING ACTS

In the process of writing this book, I learned something about myself that I don't like. I'm blessed to have priceless friendships with people meant to be around for a lifetime. Those friendships are at their peak when we can spend lots of time together. When our proximity changes, I'm rarely successful maintaining bonds in the same meaningful way. Dee was the first of a few of my sister's friends to endure this because I didn't make our relationship a priority after our zip codes changed. I take full responsibility for it. It wasn't until I wrote this book that I finally understood the *why* behind my behavior.

In Chapter One, I talk about my parents' divorce and Dad's move to Jamaica. It's my first long-distance relationship—one I don't want and completely resent. Our relationship changes so much. We're disconnected, and

I don't know my dad anymore. I hate that we're growing apart. Dad brushes it off, trying to convince me nothing has changed. We just live in different houses. His cavalier attitude is hurtful and pushes me away.

Later in life, I fail to nurture my own long-distance relationships, just like Dad. I see now, every time I move away from a friend or vice versa, I start grieving before it even happens. I carry bad memories from experiences when Dad left and expect the same outcomes. To "protect" myself from the pain and abandonment I anticipate, I opt out of the maintenance required to nurture long-distance relationships. I do the bare minimum (sometimes not even that).

When Dee and I reconnected about six years ago, she called me out like a good True Crew member would. She's happy to talk to me and upset I wasn't there when she needed me. I'm glad we're on the phone because I don't think I can look her in the eye. She's right. I own it, apologize, and regain her trust by showing up for her. Being the amazing human she is, she forgives me right away. (Thanks, Dee!)

One of my most seasoned True Crew Members is Natasha. Yes, our name is spelled the same but pronounced differently. She uses the traditional pronunciation, and family and friends call her Tasha. We meet as students at Howard University in 1992. We're good friends but don't talk much after I drop out of school following Mom's death. Tasha earns her Juris Doctor from Harvard Law School and accepts a job in Washington, DC. I'm excited to have her back. Our friendship grows, and we become like sisters.

Time flies by. Tasha marries Marcus, they buy a beautiful home, and have two children. Marcus and I grow close, too. He doesn't drive because he lost his peripheral vision after an accident many years ago. That means I have the honor of driving them to the hospital for the birth of their first child, Morgan. Then Mason, my Godson, came a couple of years later. That family is my family.

Tasha and Marcus are ready for a new home better suited for their family of four. After weighing the pros and cons of buying a larger house in the DC area, they decide to move to Charlotte, North Carolina. I cry when Tasha tells me. I try to convince her to stay and selfishly say, "The kids will forget all about me!" As they prepare to move, I grieve. Tears flow for several days. I'm unmotivated and spending too much time in bed, as if pulling covers over my head will make things better. Everything is changing. Throughout the depression, what I don't recognize is how much power I have to influence what change looks like.

After Tasha moves, I'm distant. I rarely call and don't respond when she does. Thank goodness she believes I'm worth it and puts up with me. We talk about it openly. Tasha decides to be the bigger person and lets me have my space when I need it. Once in a while, I get a mildly threatening voice mail as Tasha declares it's her third unreturned call. She worries something is wrong (she's right, but I still haven't acknowledged it). She accepts I have my "phases" (I know now those were periods of depression), and I'll resurface in time. I'm grateful Tasha never gave up on me. (Thank you, Tasha!)

My fear of abandonment from the past, untreated depression and anxiety, plus a lack of prioritization, resulted in me not always being the friend I should have been. I share my shortcomings with you, so you can do better. Maintaining friendships can be *hard*, especially long-distance ones. Yes, life will get in the way at times. Like anything else, if you want it to work, commit to it and follow through.

CREWS CHANGE

If we doin' things right, our own personal value rises. It doesn't stay stagnant. As you grow and evolve, your needs change. At times, you will outgrow a crew member, or they'll outgrow you. Can you both grow *and* stay connected? *Yes*! You'll have a small number of friends that have a permanent True Crew seat. I have some I've known since junior high school, some since undergrad, and the precious few I've gained later in life. They all bring stability, love, and support.

Other crew members will cycle in and out over time. And *that's okay*, y'all. It's expected. Know and accept it now so you can recognize times when the reason or season for that relationship has ended, and you have to let go. Be intentional and honest with yourself. Don't keep members who are not serving you well or those you can no longer serve well. Understanding relationships change helps me make tough decisions about both friendships and familial relationships.

Severing relationships with friends meant to be in your life for a specific reason or season is difficult. We don't know the relationship has a specific purpose until we've gotten down the road a bit. In my case, new friends show up at just the right moment and help me grow in ways I didn't know I needed to. We bond quickly, spending lots of time together, and I'm certain we'll be friends for a lifetime.

Things change when I recognize I'm not living in alignment with my core values or not being authentic. Doing what they want me to do rather than what I want to do. Now, I'm not talking about going to a baseball game when I really want to shop. I'm talking about stopping myself from liking someone's post on Facebook to avoid angering my friend. Or walking on eggshells to not upset one friend because I'm spending time with another. Or, experiencing a Spanish Inquisition-style line of questioning when I make a decision without their consult. I was lying to myself by pretending the behavior was acceptable. My goodness, if you can't be honest with *you*, that's a problem.

Just like with Dad, I knew I had a choice to make. We can get upset, disagree, or argue endlessly, but the person responsible for addressing mistreatment of you or your own unhappiness is *you*. And so I choose *me*. I'm grateful for what I learn from those relationships and am at peace with making the uncomfortable and unpopular choice to end them. I have no regrets.

WHAT YOUR TRUE CREW ISN'T

Your True Crew members, unless professionally credentialed as such, are not your medical doctor, psychologist, financial advisor, attorney, career coach, or relationship counselor. You can seek their guidance in any of those areas, but understand it is only that, *guidance*. If you take their advice and things don't turn out as you expect, don't blame them. *You* made a choice to follow the guidance, so *you* own the outcome. At least you know they'll have your back if something goes sideways.

KEYS TO BEING FIERCELY JOYFUL:

- 🔑 **Be authentic.** The easiest way to develop true friendships is by being yourself right from the start, including at work. Interestingly, *The State of American Friendship: Change, Challenges, and Loss*, which shares findings from the May 2021 American Perspectives Survey, states 54 percent of Americans with close friends say they met a close friend at their or their spouse's workplace (Cox 2021).
- 🔑 **Address stinky fish.** If something is bothering you, be upfront and talk to your crew about it. Stinky fish don't smell better over time. Start by expressing how their actions/language made you feel rather than accusing. I promise the conversation will be more productive without finger-pointing.

- ✒ **Set expectations.** As with any team, cabinet, or crew, it's important to set expectations. Appointing folks to your crew without giving them an assignment means you can plan on them not meeting your expectations. Need an accountability partner? An optimist? A direct truth teller? Ask and you'll receive.

- ✒ **Give and receive.** There will be times when you're doing lots of receiving, and the scales seem uneven. Though it sounds fair and balanced to say, friendships aren't a fifty-fifty thing all the time. The scales will fluctuate. You each fill the role you're needed for at the time. You'll switch to more giving than receiving when the time is right.

- ✒ **Make a plan to stay connected.** Think of it like any other goal that's important to you. Make a plan and stick to it, one task at a time. Maybe you decide on dinner quarterly for your local crew members and Zoom happy hours for the long-distance ones. Whatever works for you both, calendar it and make it happen. Be sure to include an emergency clause in your plan. For example, things happen, and you might have to miss a dinner. Make a rule that you won't miss two in a row so you can get back on schedule.

12

BE COURAGEOUS

"He who is not courageous enough to take risks will accomplish nothing in life."

—MUHAMMAD ALI

A LESSON FROM DAD

In the early 1980s, Dad decides to run for mayor of Scranton, Pennsylvania, where I was born and raised. Being a Black man running as a mayoral candidate in a majority White city, he knows he need lots of support to win over a significant number of voters. One day, he loads us all into the car, drives to Allentown, Pennsylvania, and knocks on Muhammad Ali's door. Yes, the former heavyweight boxing champion of the world my dad doesn't know and has never met.

I'm ten years old at the time, so I don't remember all the details. I definitely recall my mouth hanging wide open when Mr. Ali opens the door. Dad introduces himself and goes right into his pitch. Before I know it, we're inside the house, and Ali is doing magic tricks for us kids and agrees to campaign with Dad. *Man, what did Dad say to Ali? I mean, who does that?* Now, things have changed since then—no one is walking up to any celebrity athlete's front door in this day and age. But even then, I'm not sure I would have believed it if I didn't see it.

Ali comes to Scranton to campaign with Dad some weeks later. Lucky for me, the media follows them around everywhere, so we have newspaper photos capturing precious moments. Around midday, Dad and Ali come home for lunch. My brothers ask him for his autograph, and he happily signs a piece of paper. They take it to the library, make photocopies, and *sell them* for five dollars each! When he finds out, Ali tells them he better get his cut.

Just over 1,000 Scrantonians vote for Dad, which is less than 10 percent of the total votes cast. I hold my head down, sobbing when the election is called because I was so certain Dad was going to win. He wraps his arms around me while I tell him between sniffles that I'm sad he lost. He says, "Darling, we didn't lose. We won! This wasn't about getting the most votes. It was about letting people know what we stand for. Guess what? Now they all know!" Although Dad didn't win the election, the experience changes our lives forever. I learn you *can* win in the midst of defeat if you stay true to your values and beliefs. Dad was the most joyful loser I'd ever seen.

Boxing is already a popular sport for our family, and our love for it grows exponentially after we met Ali. I meet my other two favorite boxers, Sugar Ray Leonard and Smokin' Joe Frazier. Dad developed a lifelong friendship with Ali. They don't see each other often, but Dad made sure they stayed in touch. The last time the three of us are together is at a Congressional Black Caucus Annual Legislative Conference Gala in Washington, DC, in the early to mid-nineties. For a few short minutes, it felt like a family reunion as Dad and Ali talked, laughed, and caught up a bit. Even then, I'm still in awe my dad is cool with *the* one and only Muhammad Ali!

I GOT THIS

For years, I suppress strong desires to be active, or really to do anything involved with sports. I attribute my behavior to my challenges with my weight, which have been ongoing my entire life. Over the last ten years or so, I allow myself to be free to try things without fear of failure. I have nothing to lose! My courage helped me become a runner, a competitive tennis player, a cyclist, and a triathlete.

I recall the day in 2013 when I take my first bike ride in more than twenty years. I'm nervous as Edwaun, and I prepare to head to the Indian Head Rail Trail. I keep wondering, *Do I have everything*? I have my shiny new GT Transeo 3.0 bike and a matching helmet, gel gloves, heavily padded capri bike pants (which make me walk like a duck), energy chews, sunglasses, brand new cycling shoes, my Garmin watch, and my husband's windbreaker. Go ahead, you can laugh, but I know I'm not the only one spending way too much money "getting ready" to start a new hobby! Edwaun and I strap in our bikes on the rack attached to our SUV and hit the road. After a quick lesson from Edwaun on pushing off to start my ride (I had been starting by sitting on the seat first and then trying to balance and take off... no bueno!), he confirms I'm good to go and leaves me to fly solo. I push off and start my ride.

Stomach knots commence immediately. I inhale and exhale, calm myself down, and silently repeat *I got this*. I pedal along, and the corners of my mouth curve up when I look right and see the two-mile marker. *Wow, that was fast!* My shoulders drop, and I take in the beautiful surroundings for a moment. Crossing the roads in between each two-mile segment is clunky. I stiffen from head to toe and pray *No traffic, no traffic, no traffic* as I approach the thick white painted crosswalk lines. I don't want to stop and start again.

Just over four miles out, Edwaun passes me on his way back. I tell him I'll turn around when I hit five. On the way back, my heart rate stabilizes. I'm feeling good. I ride by a sister-friend, and she cheers me on. There's a close call when a toddler on a bike darts out in front of me. I jerk the handlebars so hard in the opposite direction it startles me. I miss the boy narrowly, but I don't panic. I focus on finishing what I started.

I'm a mile from the finish when it hits me. It's not about the clothes I'm wearing or my safety gear. What I truly needed most today is something unseen. And so the answer is yes, I have courage. I have absolutely everything I need. Mom made sure I had courage. She lived courageously and pushed me to do the same. It's *me* putting artificial limitations on myself, letting fear take over and forgetting what I'm capable of.

After my bike ride, my heart smiles first and then my mouth. *Nah. No more of letting fear get in the way. I'm li'l Sugie* (Mom's nickname was Sugie) *and I definitely got this.*

"Courage is being scared to death but saddling up anyway."
—JOHN WAYNE

Don't self-eliminate by never even entering the game. You know for sure you won't accomplish whatever you're considering if you don't bother to try. The things we're afraid to do typically don't have horrible consequences if we fail. Remember this when you find yourself trying to talk yourself out of dipping your toe in the water.

When Mom dies, I'm surprised to hear my friends tell me how much she meant to them. She made them feel loved, valued, and heard (the latter is quite interesting because she listened to our friends more than she was willing to listen to us... lol). Mom welcomed everyone with open arms... even those she thought might be trouble. She'd let them know she was always watching!

I get home, my body spent both from the ride and the nerves. After I collapse on my bed, I turn my head, look in the mirror, and see so much of Mom in my face in mine. I visualize her beaming with pride. There's my confirmation; I can never let go of the courage to try.

KEYS TO BEING FIERCELY JOYFUL:
Showing up on Ali's doorstep? Definitely risky! Yet I try to imagine our lives if Dad didn't take the risk. I wouldn't have learned so early on to lean into courage.

- 🔑 **Be courageous so you can be authentic.** To live your absolute best life, you have to push past the fear. Courage helps you be vulnerable, and you cannot be authentic until you embrace vulnerability.
- 🔑 **You get to decide your wins.** So, your courage didn't result in your expected outcome. Noted. I employed courage when I applied for an executive job the first time. I didn't get it. Yet, I had a win in my loss. If I hadn't applied, I wouldn't have learned about my sub-par interview skills. (I'm now known as the interview coach!) Each time I was told no, there was a yes meant just for me further down the road. When you miss the mark, reflect on what you learned, adapt if you need to, and celebrate you were courageous enough to try.
- 🔑 **Failure doesn't define you.** It's not who you are, it's simply what happened. How you respond to a failure matters. Anytime Dad got kicked down, he got back up still holding a glass half full. His bounce backs helped me learn to embrace failures with a positive mindset.

🗝 **Don't let your falls influence your climb.** Avoid overcorrecting because you don't want another failure. I guarantee you *will* have another failure, so expect it. Dig into your courage so you can try again, again, and again. The idea is not to throw up your hands and concede. If I gave up after years of trying to write a book with no success, you wouldn't be reading this today. It wasn't something I couldn't do. I needed to identify the *way* to do it that worked for me.

13

EMBRACE THE JOURNEY

Remember the kid in gym class who was always last to be picked for a team? That was me. Despite my lack of athleticism and body issues, I've wanted to be a runner for as long as I can remember. When driving and seeing people out running, I imagine it brings with it a sense of freedom and calm. I know... seems like an oxymoron. Moving at a high intensity and breathing heavy doesn't sound calming.

My assumption inspires my interest in running more than anything. Runners are healthy and confident, right? I don't have the courage to try it because I'm not in good shape and figure covering one block of pavement might just take me out, so I dismiss my desire.

One day, I'm speed walking on a beautiful pedestrian and bike trail in southern Maryland, the Indian Head Rail Trail, when I see two Black women jogging toward me. I smile, greet them, and cheer them on. One of the ladies, now my friend Miss Connie, says, "Come join us for a run sometime! We're with a group called Black Girls RUN! and are here this time every Saturday morning." I show up the following Saturday, and I'm hooked immediately. Before I know it, I'm running with the group several days a week and signing up for road races. In time, I become a Black Girls RUN! ambassador leading group runs, and I'm a certified Road Runners Club of America run coach offering coaching services to runners.

"We delight in the beauty of the butterfly, but rarely admit the changes it has gone through to achieve that beauty."

—DR. MAYA ANGELOU (DOUGLAS 2016, 9)

Many quotes from Dr. Maya Angelou are often repeated but not this one. I find it on May 28, 2014, the day she perishes, when I write a blog to acknowledge how much her teachings influence me.

My blog is called "Becoming Me." I've published perhaps a dozen issues over the last several years, writing when I have something meaningful to say about my personal journey becoming more of who I am meant to be. The passing of Dr. Angelou was one of those times.

At the time of Dr. Maya Angelou's passing, I'm at the peak of my amateur running career and start branching off into road cycling and triathlons. Becoming a runner, or more appropriately, an athlete, helps me develop greater self-confidence and an appreciation for not just the destination or the goal, but the journey it takes to get there.

Dr. Angelou's quote so aptly describes the culmination of my endeavors. When I post a picture of myself on

Facebook donning my medal in front of the Iwo Jima sculpture after I run the Marine Corps Marathon, my first 26.2 mile running event, I'm congratulated by so many people. There are hundreds of "likes" and dozens of comments on the picture of me crossing the finish line. But how did I get there?

I run over *650 miles* during the Summer of 2012 in preparation to run 26.2 on October 28. Throughout my training, there is too little sleep, stress about meeting race pace requirements (I'm a slow runner even at my very best!), soreness and chafing, heat exhaustion, missed social events due to scheduled long runs, a change in eating habits, friends saying I'm "doing too much," breaking up with training partners who aren't committed, significant others and loved ones who deserve more time and many more challenges.

The bottom line? Let's all be mindful of Dr. Angelou's words as we embrace our quest for living authentically. Getting there ain't so pretty. Sorry y'all, I gotta call it what it is! But wait... there's awesome news! If you truly want to live your absolute best life, you've gotta work for it. You've got to show up for yourself. I know, you're waiting for the awesome news, right? As a result of my journey, I continue to grow in character, confidence, and humility. My heart overflows with gratitude, and I share it with everyone who's willing to receive it. *The journey is what makes us butterflies* (<== awesome news).

My readiness doesn't just happen. It's the first day I run outside when I'm nearly 300 pounds and paranoid about what the drivers passing by are thinking. It's when my run pace is slower than a fast walk pace for some. It's commuting to work nearly three hours round trip on Wednesdays then going out for an eight-mile run in the dark with a bright light on my head, jumping out of my skin when I see a deer standing on the path ahead.

It's waking at 4:30 a.m. on a Saturday morning in July to finish my long run before it gets too hot. It's the "I'm kinda feelin' myself after losing forty pounds, and I run in shorts I realize one mile in are *too short*." It's a five-alarm thunder thigh fire. Do y'all know how much chafing hurts? Yikes! It's those days when my pace is still slower than the race requirement, but I keep training anyway. Then it's the day I have a twenty-mile run on tap, and everything goes wrong. I'm out of water, with seven miles to go, so I call my friend at work; she sends her husband with Gatorade, and I keep running.

Eventually, it's race day, and my body feels fantastic the *entire* time! All the work, struggle, challenges? It pays off. Pushing past those obstacles made me strong, and I became a butterfly. I am thankful to Dr. Maya Angelou for her wisdom, teaching us so much and creating a legacy helping us grow forever in all we desire to achieve. We remember her mostly for the unbelievable sacrifices she went through to leave us her legacy, but we sure do admire her butterfly beauty. May you rest in peace, Dr. Angelou.

STRUGGLE BUS

In her book *Becoming*, former first lady, Michelle Obama says, "For me, becoming isn't about arriving somewhere or achieving a certain aim. I see it instead as forward motion, a means of evolving, a way to reach continuously toward a better self. The journey doesn't end" (Obama 2018, 419).

When I ask what her journey was like toward self-awareness and self-acceptance, which is how she defines authenticity, Angela McCullough, CEO of Angela McCullough, LLC and author of *Beyond Gender and Ethnic Stereotypes: How Women of Color are Redefining Public Leadership*, simply states, "Struggle bus." She ascribes the challenges she experienced, and sometimes still does, to several factors:

- Messages in the world about who we should be
- Cultural norms about who we should be and how we should show up
- Community expectations
- Familial expectations

At the age of seventeen, McCullough decides she wants to enlist in the military. Though she's accepted into several colleges, those she's most interested in are out of her home state of Michigan. Out-of-state means a significantly higher price tag for tuition and the myriad of other college costs. McCullough is offered scholarships from some in-state schools, but "I'm more interested in being a native Detroiter somewhere outside of Michigan. The world is just like an oyster, and I'm trying to be about looking for all the pearls."

McCullough is sold on the opportunity to travel in the military and get help with the cost of her education. Her grandmother, a wise and joyful woman, cautions her. She told McCullough women who are in the military are thought to be "loose" and poor prospects for marriage. What? I've never heard that perspective. McCullough discusses her grandmother's mindset being well aligned with many women in her generation, particularly Black women who were often urged to become teachers. "That was a pivotal moment. I could have acquiesced to what she said because she had some really strong beliefs."

At first, McCullough's mother isn't on board with her plan either. She recalls the struggle of owning what she wants versus what is expected of her. McCullough summons the courage to tell her grandmother and mom, "I won't need your permission soon enough when I turn eighteen, but I prefer to have your support to do what I know is best for me." She got it.

The pivotal moment McCullough describes is a significant step toward being authentic. "Living authentically means being in tune with who you are, understanding the full spectrum of yourself, and accepting who you are today, with the understanding that you can choose to be different tomorrow if you're willing." The full spectrum? What a wonderful way to describe the complexity of us as human beings.

"The integration of our mental and spiritual selves is a constant work in progress, and, like our physical bodies, we have muscle memory. That's why I think authenticity is so important because fighting against that causes stresses in our bodies and mental challenges."

Part of our journey in authentic living includes understanding our superpowers. McCullough has many, and I've benefited tremendously from her mentorship and counsel. "I try to help other people from the space of what they are trying to accomplish, what kind of space they need to have, how can I support brilliance in them, and how can I encourage them." Now that's what I call a superpower. McCullough doesn't work from a static list of best practices she applies to everyone she supports. Instead, she recognizes the importance of tailoring her coaching to the needs of individuals.

McCullough is a change agent. Though it's been a challenging role to own over the years, she lives into her purpose and puts herself on the line to pave the way for others knowing what will come of her sacrifices. Now, that's what I call embracing the journey.

YOU GAIN RESILIENCY ALONG THE WAY
I talked to my brother Ellis Craig in preparation for writing this book for two reasons. First, the foundation of who we are comes from our parents. It helps shape us into good world citizens. Craig has a fascinating life story, having overcome many tough obstacles over years to create a life in which he thrives.

I ask Craig how he overcame challenges earlier in life. "You have to start with personal accountability. It's easy to blame someone or something because there are often multiple influencing factors. But you can't be paralyzed by factors outside of your control, right? Look in the mirror, dig down a little bit and say, what can I do to achieve the life I want?"

In talking about our upbringing, Craig asserts, "We're not new to hard work, we're not new to integrity, we're not new to giving back, we're not new to being your best version of you. Those concepts were taught in our home." When he became a United States Marine, those concepts were reinforced, and there was a focus on excellence. Craig likens learning to getting software upgrades. "You learn, you grow, repeat." Love this analogy!

Even though he had all of those tools, he struggled to execute after his honorable discharge four years later, a veteran of the Gulf War, a conflict against Iraq. While in the Marines, someone told Craig what to do and when to do it every single day. There was a regimen everyone followed. "You can lose your identity in the military." When he became a civilian again, he realized he didn't have a roadmap for what came next—finding his place in the world.

When Craig came home, he seemed like a completely different person with a chip on his shoulder. The marines taught him Americans owe him a debt for his service, which we absolutely do, though it's a debt not typically paid in a tangible way, which was what Craig expected. "I thought it would be easy to get the job I want because I had served my country." Numerous applications and interviews later, he learned the truth the hard way—no one is going to give him special consideration or move him to the front of the line.

"I reflect, do an assessment of what I've learned and the tools I have, then work to figure out what I want to do and how I can get there." It's the early nineties y'all—he couldn't hop on LinkedIn and network because it doesn't exist yet. And, what is networking anyway? It's a concept Craig had never heard of at the time (me either). He goes back to the basics of getting what he *needs* first (a la Maslow's hierarchy of needs) and then focusing on taking incremental steps to get what he *wants*.

My brother takes time to understand his passions, what he's good at, and who can benefit from his talents. "It's important I earn a good living and can live comfortably doing what I enjoy." Craig pursues a career in law enforcement. He starts as a security guard in the private sector, becomes a uniformed federal police officer, transitions to a professional job series as a physical security analyst, and now is a senior-level intelligence specialist. He accomplishes his goals with drive and self-discipline like I have never seen before or since.

Craig didn't pursue a college education, which can be limiting both based on job requirements and the perspectives of others who diminish the idea of an individual being a valuable contributor without a degree (it's quite frustrating that people judge others based on their education). "I opted to educate myself in alternative ways." I say he's a perpetual student, addicted to learning. In a good way, of course! Craig has in the neighborhood of 137 certifications in areas spanning physical security, threat analysis, operational intelligence, and much more. Okay... not quite so many, but for a good ten to fifteen years I'm confident he earned several new credentials each year. He is a graduate of numerous prominent leadership programs, including the Excellence in Government Fellows Program. Craig is also a volunteer, a coach, and a business owner.

The journey Craig took to get to where he is today was so challenging at times, I was afraid he might burn out. For years, he worked three or four jobs at a time to make ends meet. At various times he battled loneliness, anger, and frustration. I know we all deal with those emotions throughout life. What's unusual is Craig demonstrated an innate ability to use those emotions as fuel to keep pursuing his dreams. No matter how many times he was turned down for a job, treated unfairly, or overlooked because he doesn't have a college degree, he refused to give up. These days, Craig enjoys the fruits of his labor with his wife. I couldn't possibly be more proud of him, and I know Mom and Dad are too.

"It is good to have an end to journey toward; but it is the journey that matters, in the end."

—ERNEST HEMINGWAY

I learn from Craig what resilience looks like. You don't quit because you're tired, and you don't quit because it's hard. Anything worth having requires work. Now let's be real, being resilient means you have to push through some suffering. Suffering is hard. It hurts and it's uncomfortable, particularly when it endures. Adam Grant, best-selling author of *Think Again*, posted on Twitter, "Resilience is not resistance to suffering. It's the capacity to bend without breaking. Strength doesn't come from ignoring pain. It stems from knowing that your past self has hurt and your future self will heal. Fortitude is the presence of resolve, not the absence of hardship" (Grant 2022).

The first time I ran ten miles straight without stopping a single time, my body doesn't ache, but the bricks attached to my ankles get heavier with each step starting around mile seven. My breathing normalizes, no huffing and puffing. Still, fatigue numbs me from the shoulders down. Yet, I'm unwilling to stop. The conversation with myself becomes really interesting. *You've made it almost eight miles. Two more is a piece of cake in comparison. You will be so pissed with yourself for giving up now. Remember when you couldn't run even a tenth of a mile? Look at you now! You got this!*

This, friends, is the importance of mental fortitude. When your body wants to give up or when your heart says to throw in the towel, you can instruct your brain to keep going. Craig did it and so did I. My determination to do what I once thought was impossible got me through every step of each mile.

When I look back on it now, my triumphs while training, run by run, are actually the best part of it all. I'm happy when I finish on race day, but I'm fulfilled and filled with pride for staying committed and executing on my training plan. C'mon... yes, of course I missed a day here and there. I didn't say I was perfect! The important thing is not letting minor setbacks pull us off our game.

To be clear, being resilient *does not* mean you never stop. There's a difference between taking needed breaks versus giving up altogether. It's important to take time during any journey to restore yourself. Remember when I got a Gatorade delivery during my long run? My body needed a restoral of energy to continue and finish what I'd started. Without it, I mighta had to call an Uber.

KEYS TO BEING FIERCELY JOYFUL:

- **Celebrate progress.** If we only focus on the end goal, we miss all the important moments along the way. Whether you're working toward living more authentically or completing your master's degree, be intentional about pausing to celebrate incremental progress. You deserve joy throughout the journey. Make a list of milestones you want to recognize and how you'll celebrate them.
- **Lean into resilience.** Don't suppress your feelings. Holding them isn't healthy. Let 'em out constructively. And, don't stay in your feelings for too long. How long "too long" is will vary depending on the situation. If you start to withdraw, that's likely a sign it's time to come up for air. Do something for you that brings joy to help break the funk.
- **Give and remember gratitude.** When times get tough, giving to others and embracing gratitude helps

your joy endure. You'll be surprised how quickly you can reframe the challenges and get back up.

- ☞ **Don't do it alone.** We all need support when times are tough. Stay connected with your True Crew. Seek their counsel. Ask for and accept their help. Call them when it's time to vent, and maybe give them your credit card for safekeeping, avoiding too much retail therapy. *And*, call them for those milestone celebrations!

ACKNOWLEDGMENTS

Thank you to those who held me accountable, supported, and encouraged me: Edwaun, Angela, Cathy, Tom, Katrina, Michele, Demetre, Ellis, Latema, Tasha, and Sabrina.

Thank you to those I interviewed for this book. I'm grateful for your openness and authenticity. I'm honored to share your stories and wisdom.

Thank you to my colleagues and friends at work for putting up with me talking about my manuscript for months. Somehow, every conversation led back to a chapter I'd just written in the book. Thank you for a surprise celebration when I submitted my first draft—so cute that we all thought I was pretty much done at that point!

A special thanks to my Chief sisters, who helped me along the way, especially Lucy Chen. You are all fantastic.

To my writing team, thank you for guiding me through this journey. Thanks to Eric Koester for establishing a group writing program. The Manuscripts Modern Author Accelerator gave me the tools to make my dream a reality.

Thanks to my development editor, Angela Mitchell, my structural editor, La'Kisha DeVon Jordan, and my revisions editor, Allison Browning. Thank you to my marketing specialist, Michelle Pollack, for helping me exceed my presale campaign goal with a solid marketing strategy. Thank you to the entire team at Manuscripts LLC.

Thank you to everyone for believing in me. I am humbled by your support and encouragement. Thank you to those who provided feedback on early drafts of my manuscript, helping me make this book the best it can be. A special thank you to everyone who preordered a copy or copies of my book during my prelaunch campaign. You reminded me how fortunate I am to have an amazing community.

Munir Abubaker
Darryel Adams
Gioia Albi
Gary Alexander
William Allen
Nicole Allen
Jennifer Allen Tallman
Steven Bailey
Megan Bailey
Jacqueline Baker
Donna Barnaby
Robert Beck
Nicole Beckish
Michael Beckles
Shannon Ben-Yoseph
Tennille Blackwell
Wiljanda Boatwright

Danielle Boone
LaGretta Bowser
Cassandra Boyd
Dr. Jennie Byrne
Eric Cady
Dr. Maria Calhoun
Brownie Campbell
Natascha Carroll
Gwen Caudle
Lucy Chen
Tremayne Cobb
Francesca Cook
Sabrina Cooper
Christina Cox
Nicholas D'Souza
Thomas Dalzell
Matizza Davis

Debra Payne
Christina Demuth
Mark DeNicuolo
Wendy Diep
Chi Chi Donaldson
Edwaun Durkins
Disco Durkins
Adrienne Edmond
Anika Elizarov
Jennifer Ellison
Ellis Craig
Eden Ezell
Carey Fagan
Judy Farrell
Lory Ferrer
Gaylynn Fields
Jade Floyd
Joseph Fonlon
Parran Foster
Celina Frost
Nick Fuller
Stephanie Gadson
Aileen Gariepy
Connie Way Gaston
Berthienna Green
Geme Gelgelu
Maggie Geraghty
Chalese Gilmore
Tracy Giumento
Stacy Goffin
Adam Gold
Candice Gonzalez

Jonathan Gray
Miya Gray
Rebecca Guy
Katrina Hall
Stacey Hall
Vonda Hampton
Demetre Harrell-Downing
Ken Harris
Dominica Harris
Dawn Hawk
Yvonne Hawkins
Coleen Hawrysko
Dan Hicok
Dawn Hobdy
Debbie Hogan
Zena Huen
Solomon Hunter
Julie Imel
Erin Inlek
Christopher Jennison
Tatiana Jeromskaia
Tina Johnson
Karen Johnson
Tracey Johnson
Hope Johnson
Eugina Jordan
George Jordan
Cathy Kading
Christopher Kading
Nancy Kalinowski
Dacia Kelly
Miranda Kendrick

Jasmine Khan
Eric Koester
Mohammad Kushan
Yadira Lacot
LaShandel Langston
Liddia Langston
Lisa Lapp
Hyunah Lee
Yolanda Lee
Sara Levis Valvonis
Cynthia Lewis
Kim Lott
Sabrina Loving
Rob Lowe
Daren and Tina Mainer
Cheryl Major
Natesh Manikoth
Kate Marinaro
Robin Marion
Taneesha Marshall
Tamara Marsico
Jodi McCarthy
Angela Mccullough
Felicia McGinty
Elizabeth McGovern Assink
Patricia McGowan
Patty McGowan Lafferty
Natasha McKenzie
Stephanie Mcknight-Bailey
Lashante Medina
Michele Merkle
Jay Merkle

David Meusel
Ronnette Meyers
Bill Middleswart
Staci Mildenstein
Shelley Miller
Darcy & Regina Miller
Danyell Miller
Joseph Miller
Caroline Moran
Michele Murner
Stacy Murray
Angelia Neal
April Neufeld
Randy Park
Antoinette Penny
Sadie Perez
Susan Pfingstler
Jeff Planty
Gregory Pray
Crystal Pringle
Angela Proctor
Kim Pyle
Tom Rainey
Dawn Ramirez
Lynn Ray
Jenna Reese
Amber Rivera
Aretha Robinson
Nora Robson
Kimberly Rountree
Nikki Sanders
Jon Santee

Lynn Schaeffer
Jacqueline Shackleford
Kathy Simays
Leslye Sims
TuNia Slade
Karen Smiley
Calvin Brent Smith
Tamara Smith
Lenita Smith
Keith Smith
Amy Solensky
Grace Speights
Tamara Stallings
Jessica Strieter Elting
Arlene Tabares
Amy Yedinak

Talethia Thomas
LaDonna Thompson
Charles Thorpe
Laura Valero
Anna Varfolomeeva
Amanda Vincent
Dominique Wallace
Evalyne Bryant-Ward
Victoria Wei
Monte White
Staci Wilhelm
Angela Wilson
Janet Womack
Lolita Worthy
Kerryaine Yarber

APPENDIX

INTRODUCTION

Cole, Harriette. 2000. *How to Be: A Guide to Contemporary Living for African Americans.* New York, NY: Simon & Schuster.

1. BECOMING ME

Angelou, Maya (@mayaangelou). "My mission in life is not merely to survive, but to thrive; and to do so with some passion, some compassion, some humor, and some style." Facebook. July 5, 2011.

Douglas, Arthur Austen. 2016. *928 Maya Angelou Quotes.* Roosevelt, UT: UB Tech. Google Books.

2. AUTHENTICITY DEFINED

Brown, Brené. 2020. *The Gifts of Imperfection: 10th Anniversary Edition.* New York: Random House Publishing Group.

Hollis, Rachel. 2018. *Girl, Wash Your Face: Stop Believing the Lies About Who You Are So You Can Become Who You Were Meant to Be.* Nashville, TN: Nelson Books.

3. BE VULNERABLE

Brown, Brené. 2012. *Daring Greatly: How the Courage to Be Vulnerable Transforms the Way We Live, Love, Parent, and Lead.* New York: Avery.

Brown, Brené. 2018. *Dare to Lead: Brave Work. Tough Conversations. Whole Hearts.* New York: Random House.

Solomon, Lou. 2016. "Two-Thirds of Managers Are Uncomfortable Communicating with Employees." *Harvard Business Review.* March 9, 2016. https://hbr.org/2016/03/two-thirds-of-managers-are-uncomfortable-communicating-with-employees.

Warrell, Margie. 2015. *Brave: 50 Everyday Acts of Courage to Thrive in Work, Love and Life.* Australia: John Wiley & Sons Australia, Ltd.

4. GET CONNECTED

Fowley-Doyle, Moïra. 2017. *Spellbook of the Lost and Found.* New York, NY: Kathy Dawson Books.

Hubbard, Reginald. 2020. "Joyful Defiance in the Call for Courageous Action." Speech delivered October 18, 2020 via Zoom.

5. IT'S NOT ALL ABOUT YOU

Sivers, Derek. 2010. "First Follower: Leadership Lessons from Dancing Guy." Derek Sivers. February 11, 2010. 2:57. https://www.youtube.com/watch?v=fW8amMCVAJQ.

6. USE YOUR VOICE

Forliti, Amy, Steve Karnowski, and Tammy Webber. 2022. "Medical examiner: No pressure on Floyd autopsy report." *AP News.* February 1, 2022. Accessed December 3, 2022. https://apnews.com/article/death-of-george-floyd-george

-floyd-minneapolis-thomas-lane-homicide-76841a4d8c62d-
f790bad5d81b23e894d.

Grant, Adam (@AdamMGrant). 2022. "Authenticity is not about
being unfiltered. It's about staying true to your principles.
The goal isn't to voice every opinion you hold. It's to stand
up for ideas that are consistent with your ideals. Being genuine is closing the gap between what you value and what
you express." Twitter, November 10, 2022, 9:42 a.m.

Thomson, Sarah. 2020. "The Power of Being a Bit More You
How to Find and Use Your Authentic Voice and Why It
Matters." November 24, 2020 in Leicester, United Kingdom.
TEDxDMUwomen video, 12:49. https://www.ted.com/talks/
the_power_of_being_a_bit_more_you_how_to_find_and_
use_your_authentic_voice_and_why_it_matters.

Washington Post Police Shootings Database (accessed February 5, 2023). https://www.washingtonpost.com/graphics/
investigations/police-shootings-database/.

7. BE A GIVER

Brenner M.D., Abigail. 2020. "5 Reasons Why It's Important to Forgive." *Psychology Today* (blog). September 29,
2020. https://www.psychologytoday.com/intl/blog/
in-flux/202009/5-reasons-why-its-important-forgive?g-
clid=CjwKCAjwqZSlBhBwEiwAfoZUIDCo9C9gzE-
fBmnHMXeo7cQIAQUXTOtOVZ_VRob15OhgJF2HHXx-
JyRRoCRC4QAvD_BwE.

Health Essentials Staff. 2022. "Why Giving is Good for Your
Health." *Cleveland Clinic Health Essentials.* December 7, 2022.
https://health.clevelandclinic.org/why-giving-is-good-for-
your-health/#:~:text=Health%20benefits%20of%20giv-
ing&text=As%20you%20help%20someone%20or,sense%20
of%20connection%20with%20others.

Sanna, Nate. 2020. "4 Big Reasons To Put Service at The Center Of Your Life." *Age of Awareness* (blog), *Medium*. July 15, 2020. https://medium.com/age-of-awareness/4-big-reasons-to-put-service-at-the-center-of-your-life-5a9977ab8eb7.

8. BE GRATEFUL

"Giving thanks can make you happier." 2021. *HealthBeat,* August 14, 2021. https://www.health.harvard.edu/healthbeat/giving-thanks-can-make-you-happier#:~:text=In%20positive%20psychology%20research%2C%20gratitude,adversity%2C%20and%20build%20strong%20relationships.

9. POLISH YO'SELF

Hewlett, Sylvia Ann. 2014. *Executive Presence: The Missing Link Between Merit and Success.* New York, NY: HarperCollins Publishers.

Parker, Kim, Juliana Menasce Horowitz, and Renee Stepler. 2017. *On Gender Differences, No Consensus on Nature vs. Nurture.* Washington, DC: Pew Research Center. https://www.pewresearch.org/social-trends/2017/12/05/americans-see-different-expectations-for-men-and-women/.

Scott, Susan. 2004. *Fierce Conversations: Achieving Success at Work and in Life, One Conversation at a Time.* New York, NY: Berkley Publishing Group.

Strong, Elsa Powel. 2022. "The Power of Personal Presence." *Training Industry Magazine,* Summer 2022, 22. https://trainingindustry.com/magazine/summer-2022/the-power-of-personal-presence/.

10. *MOVE YOUR BODY AND EASE YOUR MIND*

Keyes, Jazz. 2019. "Slave Food: The Impact of Unhealthy Eating Habits on the Black Community." *Ebony*, June 18, 2019. https://www.ebony.com/black-health-food-diet/.

Reynolds, Gretchen. 2023. "For a longer life, afternoon exercise may be best, a large study shows." *The Washington Post*, February 22, 2023. https://www.washingtonpost.com/wellness/2023/02/22/longer-life-afternoon-exercise-may-be-best-large-study-shows/.

11. *YOUR TRUE CREW*

Cox, Daniel A. 2021. *The State of American Friendship: Change, Challenges, and Loss.* Washington, D.C: Survey Center on American Life. https://www.americansurveycenter.org/research/the-state-of-american-friendship-change-challenges-and-loss/.

Ragas, Matthew W., and Bolivar J. Bueno. 2002. *The Power of Cult Branding: How 9 Magnetic Brands Turned Customers into Loyal Followers (and Yours Can, Too!).* Roseville, California: Prima Publishing.

13. *EMBRACE THE JOURNEY*

Douglas, Arthur Austen. 2016. *928 Maya Angelou Quotes.* UB Tech.

Grant, Adam (@AdamMGrant). 2022. "Resilience is not resistance to suffering. It's the capacity to bend without breaking. Strength doesn't come from ignoring pain. It stems from knowing that your past self has hurt and your future self will heal. Fortitude is the presence of resolve, not the absence of hardship." Twitter, November 13, 2022, 2:38 p.m.

Obama, Michelle. 2018. *Becoming.* New York, NY: Crown.